POSITIVE PRACTICE

**an HVA guide to caring
for families and children
affected by HIV/AIDS**

by Robin Gorna

foreword by Claire Rayner

HVA/SHVA joint working party on HIV/AIDS
Sue Anderson (school nurse)
Sue Botes (HVA professional officer)
Elspeth Gould (health adviser)
Caroline Jacquet (health visitor)
Isobel McInnes (health visitor)
Olwen Ross (health visitor)
Debbie Timms (health adviser)

Published by
Health Visitors' Association
50 Southwark Street
London SE1 1UN

Designed by Bridget Orr
Printed by Biddles Ltd, Guildford
Cover photo by John Birdsall (library photo posed by models)
Illustrations by Anthony Lewis
ISBN 1 872278 21 3

Contents

Foreword

TEN YEARS AGO FEW people had heard of HIV infection, or of the cluster of symptoms which follow, labelled AIDS.

Five years ago all was gloom and despair as we were told that we faced a ghastly, untreatable, killing disease.

Now we're a little wiser. We know that HIV infection, while dangerous, can be prevented from spreading – if people know how, and put what we know into practice. We also know that the onset of AIDS can be held back for quite some time; that the symptoms of HIV and AIDS can be managed. We know that people with HIV and with AIDS can – and do – live full, busy and contented lives.

But more knowledge is needed, especially by those professionals who help look after adults and children with HIV/AIDS in the community: in their own homes, in baby and toddler groups, in schools and in the workplace. Such professionals have a unique opportunity to provide the best possible support because they work so closely with individuals in their chosen, familiar settings, unlike the inevitably artificial atmosphere of a hospital.

This excellent publication provides just that knowledge. It is state-of-the-art, and health visitors, school nurses and, indeed, all nurses and other carers working in the community setting will find it invaluable.

I'm delighted this book is here, and even more delighted that health visitors, school nurses and their community nursing colleagues are also here to use it.

You have so much to contribute, to all of us. Where would we be without you? And it's my guess many of you will voice the same feeling about this excellent guide.

Claire Rayner
September 1994

Introduction

THE AIM OF THIS guidance is to inform and promote good practice on HIV/AIDS for health visitors, school nurses and other registered nurses working in the community and primary health care setting.

The principles which underlie the education and practice of all registered community nurses are:

- the search for health needs

- the stimulation of an awareness of health needs

- the influence on policies affecting health

- the facilitation of health-enhancing activities.[1]

These principles are all relevant to the care of families, individuals and children affected by HIV/AIDS.

HIV is increasingly an issue for client groups served by the community nursing services, and those working in health promotion, health education and preventive health services in particular. Every member of the public needs to be aware of HIV and AIDS, and community nurses should be incorporating activities to promote this awareness among their client groups. Policies to control the spread of HIV, and the provision of services to people and families affected by HIV/AIDS, need to be appropriate and supportive. Activities to prevent HIV and to mitigate the impact of AIDS are an important aspect of public health strategies, and will contribute significantly to the well-being of individuals, families and the community at large.

This guidance concentrates primarily on the important contribution which health visitors, school nurses and other registered nurses working in health promotion and child and family health care can make to HIV prevention. It also deals with the specific needs of individuals within their client groups who are living with or affected by HIV/AIDS. It does not attempt to cover the special needs of health advisers, nor those aspects of clinical community nursing practice concerned with surgical and invasive treatments. However the basic facts and principles described here will be relevant to and provide the basis for good practice in all health care settings.

Finally, it should not be forgotten that HIV/AIDS affects every one of us, and this guidance will also be relevant to the personal and family lives of its readers.

SECTION 1

The basics

Acquired immune deficiency syndrome (AIDS) is the diagnosis used to describe an individual's medical condition when one or more of a range of opportunistic infections and tumours occur as a result of damage caused to the human immune system by the human immunodeficiency virus (HIV).

1   Defining HIV/AIDS

AIDS WAS DEFINED medically before HIV was discovered. The catalogue of clinical symptoms and conditions which define AIDS has been altered and refined as information about HIV disease has developed. Tracking the natural history of HIV in different groups of people, and among children, drug users and women in particular, and over a longer period, has revealed an enormously broad clinical picture. Increasingly doctors and researchers think of AIDS in terms of a spectrum of asymptomatic and symptomatic HIV disease, rather than a single condition.

There is usually a long asymptomatic phase, or incubation period, from the time when a person becomes infected with HIV to the development of actual symptoms associated with the infection. Some people with HIV can be very unwell without having an AIDS-defining opportunistic infection or tumour. In adults the incubation time is long: over ten years for at least half of people infected with HIV.[2] The progression tends to be much more rapid in babies born with HIV infection: one in four develops AIDS or dies within a year.[3] The life expectancy of adults with AIDS varies, depending on the nature of their first AIDS-defining symptoms. One in three people with AIDS lives for more than two years following their initial diagnosis.[2]

The precise mechanisms by which HIV causes disease (the pathogenesis) is still unclear, although there are many theories and general agreement about the basic elements. HIV is a retrovirus which damages the immune system: the mechanism by which the body protects itself against diseases. HIV replicates (multiplies) within the CD4 cells (also called T-helper cells), which are a part of the immune system. CD4 cells orchestrate the protective response when an infection enters the body. HIV multiplies throughout the CD4 cells, weakening the immune system so that the individual is unable to fight off any infections they encounter, whether new (primary) infections or old infections which are re-activated because the immune system is weak. HIV also infects other parts of the body; in particular the glands, where it 'hides' early on in infection and often leads to swollen glands (persistent generalised lymphadenopathy). As well as damaging the immune system, HIV causes direct harm to other parts of the body; in particular the central nervous system (CNS). In children the CNS, gastro-intestinal (GI) tract and lungs can be badly affected by HIV itself.

The illnesses which may occur in people with symptomatic HIV disease affect all systems of the body. Symptoms can be systemic, such as severe wasting in adults and failure to thrive in infants, or occur in specific organs. Lung conditions are frequent: for example, pneumocystis carinii pneumonia (PCP), which is one of the most common illnesses affecting people with HIV and is often the first opportunistic infection in children with HIV, especially those who become ill in the first year of life.

Increasingly doctors think of AIDS in terms of a spectrum of HIV disease, rather than a single condition.

Gastro-intestinal conditions are also common, and may be the result of pathogens such as cryptosporidia, or viruses which affect many organs of the body: for example, cytomegalovirus (CMV). CMV also causes lung disease and can lead to blindness (usually in adults). Herpes viruses such as shingles are also commonly found among people with HIV disease.

The brain may be affected by HIV, either directly or by conditions such as meningitis and toxoplasmosis. People with HIV are also prone to cancers: Kaposi's Sarcoma (KS), a cancer of the skin and internal organs, is often found in gay and bisexual men; pre-cancers of the cervix are frequent in women with HIV. Women also report severe and recurrent gynaecological conditions, including pelvic inflammatory disease (PID), and persistent vaginal thrush which fails to respond to treatment. These conditions are also common in women who do not have HIV, but they occur even more frequently in women with HIV infection.

Many of the conditions which occur in adults and children with HIV/AIDS, and the signs and symptoms associated with them, also occur in people who are not infected with HIV. It is extremely unwise to make presumptive diagnoses based upon assumptions about an individual's supposed risk of HIV. True HIV disease (symptomatic or asymptomatic) cannot be established without blood tests, and many of the conditions which may be AIDS-related will also need laboratory investigation, or examination by a doctor experienced in HIV/AIDS.

2 The impact of HIV/AIDS

THE FIRST CASE REPORTS of what is now known as AIDS appeared in the USA in 1981, when a report was published describing the incidence of a range of diseases related to immune deficiency among young, previously healthy men, in three US cities.[4] The only factor linking these men was that they were gay; hence initially the disease was called 'gay-related immune deficiency'. Soon, however, the disease was identified among haemophiliacs, drug users and people who had received blood transfusions, and it became apparent that whatever caused the condition was transmitted in similar ways to hepatitis B, through blood and sexual fluids. In 1983 French researchers identified a virus as responsible for AIDS.[5] American researchers claimed the same discovery a year later,[6] and a test became available shortly thereafter. This virus is what is now known as HIV.

The discovery of the virus associated with AIDS made it possible to identify those infected before they developed life-threatening complications. This has meant that people with HIV can be provided with appropriate and more comprehensive care before they enter a critical stage of terminal illness. It also allows a better understanding of the true impact of HIV/AIDS. Because of the time-lag between HIV infection and the development of AIDS, statistics based on AIDS cases alone can only tell us who was infected some ten years ago; HIV statistics can tell us who has been infected both in the past and more recently.

Complete and accurate information on how many people have HIV is not available, because HIV is not a notifiable disease. This is deliberate public health policy; it is considered that people will be less likely to seek testing if a condition is stigmatised by being declared legally notifiable, as is the case with many sexually-transmitted diseases, such as gonorrhoea. However we do have reliable information on the number of

HIV is not a notifiable disease. This is good public health policy, in order not to deter people from seeking testing.

people with AIDS, based on voluntary reports from doctors, although the statistics may not be fully up-to-date as there is often a time-lag in reporting.

Journalists often make the error of discussing the epidemic in Britain only in terms of known AIDS cases, and then claim that its impact is minor, and so of no great concern. This approach is dangerously misleading, since it fails to recognise two important factors: that there can be as many as ten people with HIV for every individual diagnosed with AIDS, not all of whom will be aware of their infection;[7] and that, since HIV is a transmissible infection, there is a constant potential for increased spread.

To understand the impact of AIDS, we need to know:
- how many people are known to have AIDS
- how many people are known to have HIV infection
- how many people are estimated to be infected with HIV
- how HIV is transmitted, and how easily
- the risk behaviour of people (assumed to be) infected with HIV
- how the profile of the epidemic is changing over time, and in particular the scale of its impact among identifiable groups or communities.

The numbers of people with an AIDS diagnosis and with known HIV infection in England, Wales and Northern Ireland are reported to the Centre for Disease Surveillance and Control (CDSC) in north London, and the Communicable Diseases Unit (CDU) in Scotland. Every month the CDSC releases current figures and an analysis of significant trends and developments in the profile of the epidemic. The CDSC publishes two sets of statistics: HIV infections and AIDS cases reported in the latest reporting period (the previous quarter and year), and the cumulative HIV and AIDS figures, showing the total number of cases of HIV and AIDS reported since the first AIDS case was recorded in the UK, in January 1982.

There may be as many as ten people with HIV for every individual diagnosed with AIDS, not all of whom will be aware of their infection.

Much media attention and public debate has focused on whether the early predictions about rates of increase of AIDS and HIV were accurate. Estimations made in the early 1980s were based upon very little information, and have in fact proved to be far too high. However, predictions made since 1987 have proved to be much more accurate.

A look at the 1993/94 figures gives some idea of the scale of incidence. At the end of July 1983 a cumulative total of 14 cases of AIDS was officially reported. By 31st March 1994 the cumulative total of people known to be HIV-infected was 21,670; 9,025 people in the United Kingdom had been reported as having AIDS, and of these 6,031 had died. Reported incidence of AIDS among children up to the age of 14 at 31st October 1993 was 136 cases, of whom 74 had died, and there were 436 reported cases of HIV. A total of 660 babies had been born to HIV-positive women, of which 235 were definitely infected with HIV, and 93 had subsequently developed AIDS.

Placing current figures in this context shows that AIDS is a growing problem in the UK, with a dramatic increase from those initial 14 reports. The speed of new infections and diagnoses is swift, so that statistics inevitably quickly go out of date. Local and national AIDS organisations should be contacted for details of the most recent up-date on incidence.

In addition to needing to know the total number of people with HIV/AIDS, we also need to know the spread of the disease in certain areas, and who is affected. In terms of geography, the area in and around London has the highest population of people affected by HIV/AIDS, with the north west and north east Thames regions reporting nearly half of the total known cases of AIDS in the UK. However caution should be applied when interpreting statistics about the geographical spread of HIV/AIDS, as these show only the regions where an HIV or AIDS diagnosis is reported; frequently (and this was especially the case in the early days of the epidemic) people seek medical services connected to HIV/AIDS away from their home, either in order to preserve confidentiality or because they believe that more specialised services are available where there is already a high concentration of people with HIV/AIDS. If people do live in the places where they were first diagnosed, they may often move away during the progress of the disease: for example, if they become unwell and wish to move nearer to family and/or friends. While the CDSC figures will help with planning local services, they should be supplemented by local data: for example, monitoring the numbers of people with HIV/AIDS using local services.

When profiling the people who typically present with AIDS/HIV (risk groups), it should be remembered that, while this will indicate the general pattern of the epidemic, the information is not precise. Sometimes people do not reveal full information about their risk factors at the time of diagnosis, or they may not be asked in sufficient detail about this. Detailed information on which accurately to predict the future spread of the disease is lacking, and again it is important not to make assumptions about certain groups of people: for example, many gay men also have sex with women, and not all injecting drug users are heterosexual.

Health visitors and school nurses have a special interest in families and children, in the context of the whole community, so current and projected rates of HIV infection among children and women will be most significant to their practice. Cases in women and children will indicate the extent of HIV and AIDS in families, and among people who are most likely to bear children. Some children have become infected through modes of transmission more usually associated with adults: in the past some boys with haemophilia became infected from contaminated blood in the clotting product Factor VIII; young people of both sexes may be infected through sex (both consensual and coercive), and through sharing drug injection equipment. However, the majority of children will be infected with HIV because their mother is HIV-infected, and so the progress of the disease among women is extremely important to our understanding.

As HIV/AIDS was initially detected among gay and bisexual men, and since gay men continue to bear the brunt of the epidemic, some people have considered HIV to be a disease of men. This is not the case. While HIV and AIDS continue to have a disproportionate impact among gay men and their communities, the next most vulnerable group is women who have sex with men, with whom health visitors in particular are concerned. Health visitors need therefore to be up-to-date with the statistics on the spread of the disease among women of child-bearing age, as well as incidence as a whole.

While HIV and AIDS continue to have a disproportionate impact among gay men, the next most vulnerable group is women who have sex with men.

By the end of the first quarter of 1994, the cumulative total of women known to have HIV was 2,910; 727 women had developed AIDS, and 387 had died. Most women with HIV and AIDS are aged 15-34: the peak childbearing years. Of women known to have HIV, 79 per cent are this age, and 64 per cent of women with AIDS. This is significantly younger than men: 60 per cent of men with HIV and 42 per cent of men with AIDS are aged between 15 and 34 years.

Although the absolute numbers for women are small, the potential for this increasing is real, and is already under way. Between September 1991 and August 1993 there was a six per cent increase in the number of male AIDS cases, and a 32 per cent increase in AIDS cases in women. As the numbers are still small, this can distort percentages; however these percentage increases reflect infections acquired around ten years ago, and demonstrate a significant and growing incidence of the epidemic among women. Analysis of global statistics shows quite clearly that although the ratio of men to women with HIV/AIDS started at some 8:1 (as it is in the UK), in only a few years it has moved towards a parity ratio of 1:1. Nor is there any evidence to suggest that the reality and the threat of HIV/AIDS is declining in the UK. Official statistics and anecdotal reports from health workers show that an increasing number as well as an increasingly diverse range of people are infected with HIV.

3   People affected by HIV/AIDS

MANY PEOPLE WITH HIV and AIDS, and women in particular, state that the most difficult part of learning their diagnosis is not the adjustment to the fact that it is life-threatening, but rather the fear of the stigma, prejudice and discrimination they may encounter. Clearly this has implications for both their physical and mental well-being. People with HIV who do not seek care will have a shorter life expectancy. Women in particular delay seeking care, and may be diagnosed with AIDS late in their illness. There are many reasons for this, and they include the fear of stigma and the need for confidentiality. Also services which are not accessible are of little use. In order to meet the needs of people with HIV/AIDS, services should be – and should be perceived as – non-judgemental, open and welcoming to people of all different cultural and racial groups and lifestyles.

There are many causes of the stigma surrounding AIDS. These include social and individual discriminatory attitudes to most of the identified groups of people at greatest risk of AIDS/HIV, and the high levels of anxiety which attach to anything connected with sexuality. The high public profile of HIV and AIDS, and the urgent need to discuss HIV risk behaviours, has meant that the modes of transmission are well-known. This can lead to a degree of intrusive, personal questioning by health care professionals not generally seen with other conditions. It can sometimes seem as though the primary consideration is not the care and treatment needs of the individual woman with HIV or AIDS, but the delving into her personal life to discover how she has acquired the condition. People with AIDS are often asked to account for their condition. Women who have never used drugs may be asked about the behaviour of their sexual partners, or to explain how they think they became infected. While this information may help epidemiologists and researchers, it is rarely relevant to the current health and social care needs of the individual living with HIV/AIDS. There is also the danger that such lines of questioning serve no purpose other than to satisfy the curiosity of the health professional.

Clearly the health professional should focus her skills on the needs of the client. In sensitive and personal areas such as sexual behaviour, drug use and moral beliefs, criticism may be heard where none was intended. It is essential to have an open, non-judgemental attitude to the immense variety of human experience, and to choose words carefully when asking questions or making statements. It is also essential to avoid making assumptions based on the automatic identification of an individual with the stereotypical image of the lifestyles of risk groups.

> **It is essential to have a non-judgemental, open attitude to the immense variety of human experience, and to avoid making assumptions.**

Sometimes a discussion about how they became infected with HIV can be useful for the individual. She may have specific concerns about or needs linked with the circumstances of her infection (known or unknown); she may need help to acknowledge and come to terms with a risk activity, such as drug use; she may be feeling frustration at always being mistakenly connected with a particular risk group.

It would be inaccurate and unhelpful to deny the existence of risk groups and sub-groups of people who have suffered disproportionately from the impact of HIV and AIDS. Any infectious condition will occur initially in clusters, and may then become more widespread. HIV is a recent condition, and is still clustered in the UK; but the virus is spreading increasingly beyond those communities first affected. The risk groups which have experienced the greatest impact are gay and bisexual men, people with haemophilia, intravenous drug users, and people from geographical areas where HIV is particularly common, such as some cities in the USA and parts of central Africa. In the UK, especially in some inner city areas, there are immigrant communities from some African countries (Uganda, for example) where HIV is a significant and widespread problem throughout the population. But many immigrants and refugees will have left extremely difficult circumstances in their home countries, and their move to a new country will be accompanied by acute social, practical and legal problems, as well as emotional or health concerns. The prevalence of HIV in some African countries has been used to stigmatise communities which are already isolated and experiencing hardship. There is a delicate balance between addressing the HIV/AIDS-related needs of clients and avoiding further stigma or alienating clients from services.

By no means all people from the recognised risk groups have HIV infection, and there are many people with HIV and AIDS who do not belong to these groups. It is dangerous to assume that people have HIV because of their identity or lifestyle. Such assumptions will often be inappropriate and will offend people, and can lead to a breakdown in the relationship between the health professional and client. Moreover, people from these risk groups often experience social discrimination because of their lifestyle or racial origin, and this has been intensified by panic about AIDS. This discrimination has included children being banned from schools and playgroups, and adults losing jobs and homes. HIV infection occurs not because someone belongs to a risk group, but because they practise activities which put them at risk if they also involve another individual who is HIV-infected. It is the activity, not the identification with a particular group, which makes HIV transmission a probability.

It is the activity, not the identification with a particular group, which makes HIV transmission a probability.

It is also important to bear in mind that there are no firm boundaries delineating risk groups. While a large number of people with HIV in the UK can be identified with a particular risk group, many are only connected through their past or current sexual partner, and increasing numbers have no such clear connection.

4 Transmission

HIV IS A FRAGILE virus and does not survive well out of the body. In order for HIV to be transmitted, the following conditions must apply:

● *HIV must be present.* HIV can only be transmitted from a person who is infected with the virus

● *HIV must be present in sufficient quantity.* Under laboratory test conditions, HIV can be detected in many of the body fluids. However, in practice, HIV is only present in sufficient quantity for transmission in a very few fluids. These are:

● blood (including menstrual blood)
● seminal fluid (including pre-ejaculate)
● cervical and vaginal secretions (mucous)
● breastmilk.

No cases of HIV transmission involving other body fluids have been reported, and infection is unlikely if there is exposure only to a minute quantity of any of the above fluids. However, the precise minimum quantity for infection is not known, and would be difficult to assess accurately

● *the virus has to enter the body through an appropriate route.* Intact skin is a good barrier against HIV. HIV can enter the blood directly by an invasive surgical procedure (blood transfusion or organ transplant), from contaminated injection equipment, or through an open wound or sore. It can also be absorbed into the bloodstream through the mucous membranes in the rectum, vagina, urethra, and under the foreskin. This can occur whether they are damaged or not, although transmission is more likely if these membranes are damaged.

These factors can be summarised as:

● quality
● quantity
● route.

HIV is transmitted through three principle routes:

● unprotected sex

● blood contact (primarily through injected drug use)
● mother–to–baby contact (both antenatal, and postnatally through breastfeeding).

4.1 **Sex**

Some people find it difficult to discuss sex, but since unprotected, penetrative anal or vaginal intercourse is the main route for HIV transmission, it is an issue which has to be addressed in HIV/AIDS care and prevention. Many HIV-positive people may have concerns and questions about the implications of their diagnosis for their sex lives, and may want to discuss this with health professionals. In addition, HIV can only be prevented if people fully understand which sexual activities place them at risk and how to avoid infection, and health visitors, school nurses and practice nurses have a crucial role here.

Given the taboos in our culture against talking about sex, many of us – health professionals and clients alike – have difficulty in finding the best language to use. It can be embarrassing and awkward to talk about sex, and this may be made more difficult if we do not understand the words that are used. Humour never hurts, and may offer a good way to begin talking about sex. When discussing any difficult topic, health visitors and nurses should be guided by their clients' level of understanding and language, and it may help to experiment with alternative words for sexual acts and parts of the body, in order to find those which are more appropriate to the client's lifestyle, or less complex and more precise than strict medical terminology.

HIV can only be prevented if people fully understand which sexual activities place them at risk, and how to avoid infection.

It is essential to avoid language which clients find offensive or unacceptable, but if a client is more comfortable with vague language such as 'making love' or 'sleeping together', it is important to find out what they mean by these terms. Often it helps to try out different terms to ensure that the client understands and to find the language with which they are most at ease.

4.1.1 *Penetrative sex*

Women have become infected by HIV in seminal fluid entering their bodies through mucous membranes in the anus, vagina or cervix. Men have become infected by HIV in blood, menstrual blood, vaginal and cervical secretions entering their bodies through mucous membranes in the urethra or under the foreskin, or from semen in the anus.

Cuts, abrasions, inflamed areas or ulcerative lesions will increase the likelihood of acquiring HIV.

The presence of cuts, abrasions, inflamed areas or ulcerative lesions (caused, for example, by sexually transmitted diseases) will increase the likelihood of acquiring HIV. Other factors which can enhance the likelihood of transmission include the specific strain of the virus; the stage of HIV disease (infectivity is highest immediately after infection and when a person is ill); whether either person has a sexually-transmitted disease (STD); if the man is un-circumcised, and if there is little or no lubrication during sex, when the friction of intercourse can cause abrasions and cuts.

In general, the concentration of HIV is highest in blood, then semen, menstrual blood, cervical secretions and vaginal secretions, with corresponding descending order of infectivity. This, combined with the fact that there is a greater surface area of mucous membrane in the vagina, cervix and anus than in the urethra, means that the risk of transmission is greater to the receiving partner than the inserting partner. However, men (the inserting partner) have acquired HIV from penetrative anal and vaginal sex with HIV-positive women and men, and this is a significant route for transmission of the virus.

The mucous membrane of the anus is more fragile than that of the vagina. Further, the anus does not lubricate like the vagina during intercourse, so abrasions and cuts during anal intercourse are relatively common. This means that anal intercourse has a higher risk of transmission than vaginal intercourse. Yet most HIV-positive women say they have never had anal sex, and it is clear that vaginal intercourse is without doubt a high risk activity for HIV transmission.

4.1.2 *Non-penetrative sex*

Sex is far more than vaginal and anal intercourse. There are many other sexual activities which people find pleasurable. No other sexual act carries the same level of HIV risk as penetration of the anus or vagina without using a condom. It is perfectly safe to kiss, lick, stroke, cuddle, massage, masturbate, fantasise, or play sex games; the list is endless. HIV can only be transmitted when HIV-infected blood, semen, menstrual fluid, vaginal juices or breast milk enter the bloodstream.

In all forms of non-penetrative sex, general rules of sexual hygiene are important. It is advisable not to put anything (finger, penis, sex toy) in the anus and then the vagina, as this can transmit bacteria. Similarly, sex toys should not be shared without washing them in between use by each partner, or a new condom used (if possible) for each person. Care should be taken with any sexual practices that cause wounds or draw blood, and blood, semen and vaginal secretions should not enter any open wounds.

People who know they have HIV may want to take care with some sexual activities which could expose them to other pathogens, or to exposure to new STDs. Rimming (licking the anus) may involve exposure to bacteria in faeces. The risk can be reduced by using dental dams (or cling film). It may be best not to ingest urine since there is a risk of cytomegalovirus (CMV) infection, although this is a common virus to which most people are exposed early in their lives.

Partners who are both HIV-positive may not wish to practise safer sex, despite indications that frequent exposure to new strains of HIV may be harmful and speed up disease progression. For women, there is also the risk of increasing the gynaecological complications of HIV through acquiring STDs, including wart virus. However for some people these risks are more acceptable than adopting safer sex. This must, of course, be an individual decision.

4.1.3 *Oral sex*

A very small number of cases of HIV transmission during

oral sex have been reported, although the reliability of some of these reports is doubted. There are more reports of men and women acquiring HIV from fellatio (sucking a penis to ejaculation) than from cunnilingus (licking the clitoris, vulva and vagina). However, the total number of cases is still very small compared to the proven risks of HIV transmission during anal and vaginal intercourse. The risks of HIV acquisition are higher if someone has cuts or ulcers in their mouth, or unhealthy gums, and is the active partner doing the licking or sucking.

The factors which increase the infectivity of HIV (described above) may also be relevant. Since semen and menstrual blood have higher concentrations of virus, it may be unwise to allow these fluids to get into any cuts or wounds. However infected sexual fluids are not thought to be a risk if they enter a healthy mouth, since saliva has a disinfectant, inhibitory effect, and the acidic gastric juices will also kill HIV. There are no HIV risks from receiving oral sex (being sucked or licked) from a person with HIV.

There is some risk of transmission if the active partner (the partner doing the licking or sucking) does not have intact skin in and around the mouth. In this situation, it is advisable to avoid ejaculation in the mouth, or for the man to wear a condom. For cunnilingus during menstruation, some people have suggested using a dental dam (a square of latex), cling film, or a cut up condom or latex glove to cover the vulva. Since the risk from oral sex is so low, and unproven, it will be up to the individual to decide whether such measures need to be taken, based on what she or he considers an acceptable level of safety. However, using dental dams or condoms for oral sex may be helpful for people with oral herpes (cold sores), since this can easily be transmitted and lead to genital herpes, which is far more infectious than HIV.

It is important to remember that any risk of HIV transmission through oral sex is far less than through penetrative anal and vaginal sex. Over-emphasis on these small risks may lead people to disregard the greater risks of penetration, and to take the view that: 'If everything is unsafe, I might as well do everything'. Oral sex is certainly less risky than penetrative sex, but it is not 'safe sex' in the way that masturbation, kissing and other forms of non-penetrative sex are.

4.1.4 *Condoms and lubricants*

The correct use of a reliable condom and water-based lubricant is the mainstay of safer sex. Condoms (sheaths) should carry the British standard BS 3704 kitemark, and should be within their sell-by date. For anal sex, strong condoms are recommended, and these can also be used for vaginal sex. Anal sex is common not only between men but also between men and women: some studies have suggested as many as 61 per cent of women have had anal sex.

Over-emphasis on small risks may lead people to take the view that: 'If everything is unsafe, I might as well do everything'.

Condoms are not 100 per cent effective as a contraception, the main reason for this being user failure: that is, the condom is put on incorrectly, slips off or breaks. There have been no reported cases of HIV transmission when a condom breaks, but clearly this would reduce the efficacy. Just as women need to be shown how to insert and use the diaphragm, men and women who use condoms need to become familiar with their correct use.

Condoms should be used only once. For anal sex it is important to use plenty of lubricant, and it is often a good idea to use some for vaginal sex. If there is not enough lubrication the friction of intercourse can cause condoms to break. Misunderstandings about lubrication and vaginal sex are common. It is not a sign of failure if a woman uses a lubricant. After the menopause, and at certain times in the menstrual cycle, many women produce little natural lubrication. If the vagina (or anus) is dry, the risk of abrasions, and consequently of HIV transmission, increases.

Lubricants should always be water-based (KY jelly, for example, but there are several commercial brands), or contain sensitol or other such substance which will not destroy the latex. Many water-based lubricants (including those used on pre-lubricated condoms) contain spermicides such as non-oxynol 9. It has been suggested that these chemicals will de-activate HIV should the condom break or come off and there is a spillage. These should not be used, however, if either person is allergic or sensitive to such chemicals, as the inflammation caused by this sensitivity can make transmission of the HIV virus more likely. Using non-oxynol 9 can also cause thrush; again, in this situation it should not be used as this would enhance the vulnerability to acquiring HIV infection. Oil-based lubricants damage latex and should never be used with latex condoms. Alternative, commonly-used oily lubricants include a number of commercial products, as well as vaseline, baby oils, massage oils and cooking oils.

Correct use of a reliable condom and water-based lubricant is the mainstay of safer sex.

A relatively new prophylactic is the female condom (sold in the UK under the brand name of Femidom). It looks like a combined diaphragm and male sheath, but is larger than the male condom (the circumference is the size of a diaphragm) and has a ring at each end. The inner ring at the top helps with insertion and holds the female condom in place around the cervix (like the diaphragm). The outer ring is at the open end of the device and remains outside the vagina.

The femidom is made of polyurethane, and so can be used with any lubricant (oil does not destroy the integrity of polyurethane as it does with latex). In theory the femidom can be washed and re-used, although the manufacturers do not recommend this. Research so far suggests that the female condom is technically as effective as the male condom for preventing pregnancy, and as a safeguard against HIV and other STDs.[8] As with the male condom, however, there are concerns about its acceptability. These concerns centre on the unappealing sounds it can make when used; the look (the outer ring may hang down beyond the labia in some women); the fact that the outer ring may cover the clitoris (although some women report that it provides additional stimulation); the price; difficulties with insertion, and the fact that it needs a high degree of compliance from the male partner.

Research is under way to develop a truly female-controlled barrier, such as a cream, pessary or gel which would be sufficient on its own to de-activate HIV. At this stage, however, none has been developed. Women who are concerned about acquiring HIV but are unable to persuade their partners to use male or female condoms might gain some protection from using a diaphragm and spermicide containing non-oxynol 9, if they are not

— HOW TO USE A CONDOM —

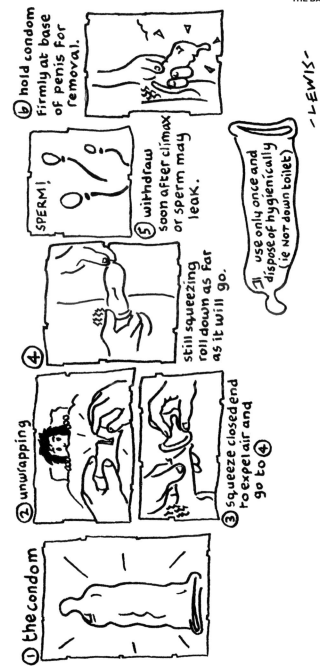

① the condom

② unwrapping

③ squeeze closed end to expel air and go to ④

④ still squeezing roll down as far as it will go.

⑤ withdraw soon after climax or sperm may leak.

SPERM!

⑥ hold condom firmly at base of penis for removal.

⑦ use only once and dispose of hygienically (ie NOT down toilet)

—LEWIS—

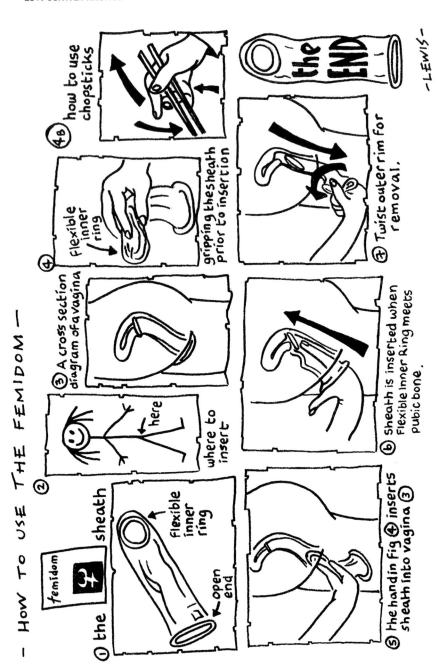

- HOW TO USE THE FEMIDOM -

① the femidom ♀ sheath
Flexible inner ring
open end

② where to insert → here

③ A cross section diagram of a vagina

④ Flexible inner ring / gripping the sheath prior to insertion

④B how to use chopsticks

⑤ the hand in Fig ④ inserts sheath into vagina ③

⑥ Sheath is inserted when Flexible inner Ring meets pubic bone

⑦ Twist outer rim for removal.

the END

-LEWIS-

sensitive to this chemical. However, this is not as effective as a condom and should only be advised as a last resort.

4.2 **Drugs**

The principle transmission route for HIV in blood-to-blood contact is through injected drug use, although a significant number of people were infected in the early days of the emergence of AIDS/HIV when they received transfusions of infected blood and/or blood products.

Drugs do not cause AIDS. The reasons why we discuss drugs in the context of HIV and AIDS are:

- HIV can be transmitted if two or more people use the same equipment to inject drugs
- the effects of the drug (or alcohol) may cause the individual(s) to be less likely to take safer sex precautions
- people who are dependent on drugs, especially drugs which are illegal, may trade sex for those drugs or money. Sex workers who are dependent on drugs may be more vulnerable to abuse and less able to insist on safer sex.

HIV is transmitted through shared drug injection equipment when at least one of the people using the equipment is HIV-infected. After they have used the works (the syringe, needle and other equipment used to inject drugs), any blood on the tip of the needle, in the syringe or elsewhere can be transferred to another person using the works.

There are many different kinds of mind-altering substances, both legal and illegal. Legal drugs include alcohol, nicotine, caffeine, solvents and prescribed medication. Illegal drugs include cocaine, heroin, marijuana, LSD, ecstasy and illegally-acquired prescribed medications. The most commonly-used injected drugs are heroin, cocaine and benzodiazepines. Some people are dependent on, or addicted to, the substances they use; others can be said to abuse or misuse drugs; and others simply use them. There are many reasons why people use drugs, and these reasons may change for an individual over time. Not everyone who uses drugs wants or needs to change their drug use. Not everyone using drugs is necessarily addicted to them, and many do not regard their use of drugs as a problem.

In terms of HIV, the primary concern is shared injecting equipment. Works may be shared by people who are dependent on drugs, but they can also be shared by those who only inject occasionally. There is a misleading tendency to label everyone who injects drugs as an 'addict' or 'misuser'. These terms are value judgements, and often do not describe the reality of the situation. Not all people who use drugs by injection are mis-using them; nor are they all dependent or 'junkies'. Such terms exclude people who inject drugs only occasionally, and may alienate them so that they receive less information than those who are dependent on substances, because they do not perceive that warnings about HIV risks and drug use apply to them. Further, professionals may omit to give appropriate health advice to those at risk if they only offer information about the dangers of sharing drug injecting equipment to people who are clearly 'addicts'.

4.2.1 *Safer drug use*

The only effective way to ensure that HIV is not transmitted through shared drug-injecting equipment is for every individual involved to use clean works. In many parts of the country clean injecting equipment can be obtained from special needle exchange projects and from needle exchange pharmacy schemes. Many drugs services offer health education on safer injecting practices, including how to avoid infections and tissue damage. Local AIDS organisations will have details about such services in your area.

As injecting can lead to other health problems (for example, septicaemia), it is advisable for each person to use their injecting equipment once only, or to find other ways to take the drugs. Most drugs which are injected can also be taken by smoking, snorting or ingestion, although some drug users do not like these methods since the quality of the sensation is different. Users of heroin and similar opiates who want to stop injecting can be prescribed methadone (a syrup substitute). Replacement or pure substances can also be prescribed medically for people who use other injected drugs, such as cocaine and benzodiazepines, and who want to minimise the harms associated with their drug use.

Stopping sharing drug injecting equipment may not be possible for some people. It may be impractical, because of lack of access to clean equipment (they may, for example, be in prison); it may not be a priority (for example, if someone is suffering from withdrawal symptoms and desperately needs the drug). Some drug users may choose to share works as part of the ritual, or as a symbolic act to signify friendship.

Terms such as 'drug addict' or 'misuser' are value judgements which exclude – and may alienate – people who inject drugs only occasionally but who are equally at risk.

There are ways to minimise the risk from sharing works, by sterilising equipment between use. Works which will withstand heat can be sterilised by boiling. Injecting equipment can be cleaned by flushing the needle and syringe with bleach. The works should be flushed through with the bleach three times, and then flushed through six times with cold water, to remove all traces of the bleach. Where bleach is not available, flushing with cold water and ordinary washing-up detergent will have some effect. However these methods are not as effective as hospital sterilisation procedures, and can only be said to reduce the risk, not remove it. Local drugs advice services and community drugs teams will be able to offer comprehensive information about reducing the harms associated with drugs use.

4.3 **Mother–to–baby**

Transmission of HIV from mother to baby is known to occur in three ways:
- *during pregnancy*, when the fetus may be infected by HIV in the mother's blood crossing the placenta
- *during delivery*, when the infant may be infected by HIV in the mother's cervical secretions or blood during the birth process
- *through breastfeeding*, when the infant may be infected by

HIV in the mother's breastmilk, or in blood taken in from cracked nipples during breastfeeding.

In European countries around 14 per cent of babies (one in seven) have become infected with HIV during the course of the pregnancy or during the birth process. A further 14 per cent of infants (one in seven) have acquired HIV from breastfeeding. An infant whose mother herself becomes infected during delivery or when she is breastfeeding stands a higher chance (some 30 per cent) of acquiring HIV from breastfeeding.[9] Research into transmission between mother and baby has developed rapidly in recent years, and continues to establish new findings. The overall rates are much lower than was first assumed, and vary widely between different geographical areas of the world, depending on how common it is for women to breastfeed, and other social, cultural and environmental factors.[10]

4.3.1 *Inter-partum transmission*

In the womb the fetus is connected to the mother by the placenta, but their bloodstreams are separate. Sometimes HIV crosses the placenta and infects the fetus. Precisely how and when this transmission occurs during pregnancy is not yet fully understood, but tests carried out on aborted fetuses suggest that it could occur as early as 12 weeks. HIV transmission in the womb may be more likely if the woman has low CD4 cell counts, p24 antigenaemia (proteins of infectious viral material), other infections (including STDs), or has AIDS. It may be advisable, therefore, for a woman with HIV who wants a child to conceive as soon as possible, before her disease progresses.

4.3.2 *Intra-partum*

Newborn infants may be infected during birth by prolonged exposure to HIV in their mother's blood, cervical and vaginal secretions. Some studies suggest that caesarean section is less risky than a vaginal delivery,[10-12] others that invasive procedures (forceps, suction caps and perhaps episiotomy) are linked to higher rates of transmission.[13] Transmission at birth is also associated with the immunological and clinical factors relating to the risk of transmission in the womb.

Where possible, HIV-positive women should avoid invasive birth procedures. It should not be assumed that all HIV-positive women will give birth by caesarean section. The difference in risk may be small, and caesarean sections are of themselves traumatic interventions, with additional health risks unrelated to HIV. It should be for the individual woman to decide for herself, on the basis of the evidence currently available.

4.3.3 *Breastfeeding*

It is now confirmed that, unfortunately, breastfeeding poses a significant risk of transmission to babies born to women with HIV.[9] Infants can become infected during breastfeeding from HIV in the breastmilk, and from blood from bleeding or cracked nipples or breast abscesses. The young, non-intact skin in the infant's mouth makes the baby more vulnerable to acquiring the virus. Research indicates that concentration of HIV may be particularly high in colostrum.[3]

In addition to the immunological and clinical factors linked to transmission in the womb and at birth, transmission is clearly associated with recent infection: that is, women infected with HIV during the third trimester of pregnancy or during breastfeeding.[12,13] Since is not possible to identify at birth which infants are already HIV-infected, all HIV-positive mothers are advised not to breastfeed where adequate alternatives, including access to appropriate formula milks and a clean water supply, exist. World Health Organisation (WHO) guidelines[14] state that the risks to an infant's health from bottle feeding in areas where the water is likely to be contaminated are higher than the risks of HIV infection from breastfeeding, and that HIV-positive women should only be advised against breastfeeding where bottle feeding carries little general health risk.

5 Infection control

IT IS POSSIBLE TO engage in very intimate activities with a person with HIV and not become infected. That the most intimate activities (such as sexual intercourse) do not always result in HIV transmission suggests that HIV is not easily transmitted. This conclusion is reinforced by the basic science of HIV, which tells us that HIV is only found in sufficient quantities for transmission in:

- blood
- seminal fluid
- cervical and vaginal secretions
- breastmilk,

and that sufficient quantities of one of these HIV-infected fluids have to pass into the recipient's bloodstream for infection to occur. These basic facts about transmission are essential for an understanding of effective infection control in clinical practice.

Health professionals face a number of health and safety hazards in the workplace, and high standards of general hygiene and infection control should always be in place. Standards of hygiene are needed not only to protect the health professional but also to ensure that the patient is not exposed to any health hazards, especially when they are immuno-compromised, as with someone with HIV, and therefore less able to fight off infections. All community nurses should be aware of and follow their employer's (or school's) policy on safe working procedures, and draw attention to any deficiencies in it, or in the equipment provided for their use.

An individual's HIV status is rarely known by the health professional; often the individual herself is unaware that she is HIV-positive. Universal infection control precautions should be applied to all patients and clients: those known to be HIV-positive, those whose status is unknown, and those who were HIV-negative when tested, and in all clinical settings.

The term 'universal precautions' is that used by the health and medical professions to describe Department of Health recommended procedures for preventing infection by diseases transmitted in blood or body fluids.[15] Universal precautions are aimed at protecting the client or patient from any pathogens (including any which may be dangerous to a person with a compromised immune system), and guarding against the transmission of HIV and other pathogens from the patient or client to the health professional.

Universal precautions are essentially good hygiene in practice. The basic principles comprise:

- wash hands after each contact
- cover cuts and grazes with waterproof dressings
- seek advice from the occupational health department if the practitioner has any skin problems
- wear single-use disposable gloves to perform procedures where there is a likelihood of contact with blood or body fluids, and disposable mask, eye protection and plastic apron if there is any risk of splashing
- do not re-sheathe used needles, and place directly into the sharps container
- dispose of all clinical waste with care, in line with local policies and procedures
- take great care with, and seek to minimise wherever possible the handling of needles and sharp instruments.

There is absolutely no need or justification for wearing full protective clothing in any but the most extreme situations where there is likely to be a lot of blood or body fluid involved. For example, to take blood it is only necessary to wear disposable gloves. Each situation should be individually assessed for its relative risk,[16] and appropriate precautions taken accordingly.

As previously stated, HIV is a highly fragile pathogen and thus less readily transmitted than many other pathogens such as, for example, hepatitis B. Infection control measures which guard against hepatitis transmission will protect against the transmission of HIV infection. However the hepatitis B vaccination does not confer immunity to HIV.

Health professionals face a number of health and safety hazards in the workplace, and high standards of general hygiene and infection control should always be in place.

Transmission of any pathogen, including HIV, in the clinical setting is rare. Universal precautions should be a feature of good health care practice with all patients, but should not interfere with the relationship between the health professional and client or patient. The additional factor of social stigma in relation to HIV and AIDS must be taken into consideration when assessing the appropriate level of precautions to take. For example, wearing latex gloves may not be necessary in all cases, and to do so may increase the client's or patient's sense of isolation.

HIV is not transmitted by coughing, spitting or biting. Nor has anyone ever contracted HIV from touching, hugging, kissing or cuddling an HIV-positive adult or child. There is no risk from children playing together. HIV is not transmitted through normal household contact, including using the same crockery and cutlery, and sharing bathroom facilities. You cannot acquire HIV from toilet seats; nor from the shared use of towels.

HIV is not transmitted by coughing, spitting or biting. Nor has anyone ever contracted HIV from touching, hugging, kissing or cuddling an HIV-positive adult or child.

Infection control precautions will vary according to circumstances and settings. In medical, surgical and clinic settings precautions will need to be more stringent, since the potential for cross-infection and exposure to multiple pathogens is higher than in, say, the home or school setting. The basic rules of *quality, quantity and route* should be applied to assess the risks of exposure and transmission in unusual situations.

5.1 Practice nurses

HIV infection control guidelines for practice nurses will also be relevant to health visitors, school nurses, and all other nurses working in clinical settings in the community.

The first principle is to ensure that infection cannot enter the bloodstream. Intact skin is an excellent protection against HIV. Where skin is not intact (for example, fresh or open wounds), waterproof plasters should be used to cover the broken skin. Large wounds on the fingers may be covered with finger cots. If the integrity of skin is severely damaged (by conditions such as eczema, for example) latex gloves should be worn. In situations where body fluids are routinely handled, latex gloves should be worn, and new gloves should be used for each patient. Regular hand washing when removing gloves, after handling body fluids, and between patients is good practice and should be routine, to protect the patient against cross-infection with other conditions.

It is advisable to wear latex gloves to clean up any spillage of blood or sexual fluid. Spilled blood should be covered completely by sodium dichloroisocyanurate granules, or covered with paper towels, and a 10,000 ppm sodium hypochlorite solution then poured gently over the spillage and the surface wiped with a disinfectant fluid. In the rare situations where splashing with blood is possible (for example, invasive surgery), goggles may be worn to protect the mucous membranes of the eye. This is not necessary as a routine precaution, however, and it is extremely unlikely to apply in most general practice, health visitor or school settings.

Needles, syringes and other sharps should be used once only. They should be handled with caution and always disposed of immediately after use, without re-sheathing (this exposes the handler to additional risk of accidental needle-stick injury). A secure, puncture-proof sharps container should be kept close to where sharps are used: for example, on the desk or immediately next to where the procedure takes place. It should be out of the reach of children. Used sharps should never be placed on a tray and then carried to another area or room for disposal. Transportable and clinic sharps containers are now available in all sizes. Sharps containers and materials (for example, towels, cotton wool) containing body fluids should be yellow-bagged and incinerated.

A health professional who suffers a needle-stick injury should immediately cease the procedure. Bleeding should be encouraged and the wound should be washed with plenty of water. The injury should be reported to your manager who will follow the agreed local reporting and follow-up procedure.

Cases of needle-stick injuries where the patient is known to be HIV-positive have been closely monitored internationally. Such incidents range from light injuries with a needle-stick to more

serious accidents where health professionals have injured themselves with surgical instruments. A review in the UK has shown
that just 0.38 per cent of health professionals have acquired HIV
following accidental exposure to HIV-infected fluids in the course
of their work.[17]

The procedure for taking blood should be the same for all
patients, whether known to be HIV-positive or not. A sterile, disposable needle should be used and gloves should be worn. Ideally,
needles should not be re-capped, but should be placed immediately
in the sharps container. When using a vacutainer, where the needle
has to be re-sheathed before unscrewing, this should be done with
great care. The blood sample should be sent to the laboratory in a
plastic bag. Some authorities require a 'biohazard' label to be used
for blood thought likely to be HIV-contaminated (with HIV antibody tests, for example, or where the patient/client is known to be
at high risk of being HIV-positive).

When taking a cervical smear or high vaginal swab, again
the procedure should be the same for all patients, regardless of their
known HIV status. Gloves should be worn. The speculum should
be decontaminated after use by washing in hot soapy water, preferably not in the basin used for hand-washing. It should be left to dry
before being sterilised in the autoclave.

5.2 Health visitors

These guidelines refer mainly to health visiting practice in
the home and child health clinic setting. They include guidance
which the health visitor may use to advise clients on infection
control measures at home if they or other household members are
HIV-infected.

It is advisable to wear household (or latex) gloves to clean
up any spillage of blood or sexual fluid. Where gloves are not available, towels or absorbent material should be used to mop up the
fluid. The surface should be wiped with a disinfectant fluid, such as
bleach, although care should be taken in the home to use bleach
only to clean surfaces it will not damage (lino or tiled floors, for

example). Hot water with washing-up detergent is an effective alternative for cleaning surfaces and materials likely to be damaged by bleach, such as soft furnishings.

Wearing gloves to clean up faeces, urine and vomit is also advisable and good hygiene practice, although these do not contain sufficient HIV to be a risk. Bleach or hot, soapy water can be used to clean the surface as appropriate.

Soiled clothing and linen can be washed normally, with detergent and hot water. Used tampons can be flushed down the toilet. Used sanitary towels, nappies, condoms and other materials containing body fluids (towels and cotton wool, for example) can be disposed of in household rubbish. Ideally, these materials should be double-bagged. Yellow-bagging is not essential, and is likely to be resisted by most patients receiving care at home, because of the social stigma it may attract.

Families with an HIV-positive child should not be excluded from services that are universally available to all children.

Where needles or a Hickman line are being used in the home setting, it will be necessary to have a sharps container and to arrange for this to be collected for incineration. The sharps container should be kept close to where the procedure takes place, and must be safely out of the reach of children.

It is not necessary to wear gloves when handling HIV-positive babies, when changing nappies, or when assisting with breastfeeding. Wearing gloves for such procedures may be very upsetting for the client, and will promote a false understanding of the infectivity of HIV.

Anyone with severely broken skin (for example, people with eczema) should not clear up spillages of blood or other body fluids unless gloves are available. A person who knows they have HIV may prefer to clean up their own body fluids, but should not be expected to do so. This is, of course, not possible where the individual concerned is an infant, or is unwell.

HIV-infected babies are particularly vulnerable to acquiring infections. Most child health clinics ask parents not to bring in children who may be unwell, and to take them to see the GP instead. This is basic good practice, and should be the accepted procedure in all child health clinics. Families with an HIV-positive child should not be excluded from services that are universally available to all children.

If any child urinates in the weighing pan, the pan should be cleaned with hot soapy water or disinfectant before the next child is weighed. Thrush can be transferred between infants as a result of not cleaning the weighing pan, and this can pose a particular risk to the HIV-infected child.

5.3 School nurses

These guidelines include information which the school nurse may be called upon to give to teachers and parents seeking their advice, and should be part of the school infection control policy. School nurses working in clinical settings should also refer to the guidelines for practice nurses.

Offering first aid assistance is an extremely low-risk activity. Following the basic rules of universal infection control should be sufficient to avoid the transmission of HIV. First aid boxes should contain gloves, although ideally anyone assisting will have covered their own wounds. Some schools expect dinner ladies and staff supervising sports always to carry gloves in their pockets. In situations where it is not possible to use gloves immediately, blood on hands should be washed off with soap and water, and mucous membranes should be splashed with plenty of cold water. With small wounds, the casualty may be able to minister to themselves under the first aider's supervision. Great care should be taken where broken glass or other sharp objects are involved.

Mouth-to-mouth resuscitation only presents a risk if the casualty is bleeding copiously and the first aider has open wounds around the mouth. In this situation, if possible, a person with intact mouth skin should offer assistance. Alternatively, disposable resuscitation equipment could be used by trained personnel. Failing this, it may be some help to place tissue or light material between the mouths. Mouth-to-mouth resuscitation is a life-saving intervention; the risk of HIV transmission is only theoretical.

Needles, syringes and other sharps should be used once only. Sharps should be handled with care and disposed of in a secure, puncture-proof sharps container. Transportable sharps containers are now widely available, but where, for some reason, a sharps container is not available, sharps can be placed in an empty drinks can. The can containing the used sharps should be flattened after use, as a further safety precaution.

Offering first aid assistance is an extremely low-risk activity. Following the basic rules of universal infection control should be sufficient to avoid the risk of HIV transmission.

The same approach to treating sports injuries should be adopted for all children, regardless of their HIV status. The person attending to the child should ensure that any cuts or wounds of their own are already covered by waterproof plasters. If not, or they have eczema, gloves should be worn. The child should be taken off the pitch and attended to, and she should not return to the game until the wound has been properly dressed and covered with a waterproof plaster. Injuries should never be sponged down with cold water from a communal bucket.

6 Testing for HIV

PEOPLE WHO ARE INFECTED with HIV are often described as HIV-positive (generally referred to as HIV+), or antibody positive. This is because the usual, most reliable, and least expensive test to establish if a person has been infected with HIV is to establish if they have antibodies to HIV in their blood.

When the body is exposed to any pathogen, the immune system produces antibodies. In most cases these antibodies help to fight the pathogen and prevent, or lessen, the illness it may cause. These are known as 'protective antibodies'. Since the direct effect of HIV is to inhibit the immune system from functioning properly, HIV antibodies do not have this protective effect. HIV antibodies are therefore simply markers, showing that a person has been exposed to a sufficient quantity of the virus for the immune system to mount a response. It does not mean that their body has been able to fight off the HIV infection.

In the UK two forms of test are used: the ELISA and the Western Blot. If blood shows a positive result on one system, a second, 'confirmatory test' is carried out using the other method, to ensure there has not been a mistake. Where the first test produces a negative result, this is considered sufficient to establish the individual's negative HIV status.

As with all pathogens, the immune system starts to produce antibodies immediately following exposure. With HIV it takes, on average, six to 12 weeks for the body to produce enough antibodies for the test to detect. This period of sero-conversion is often referred to as the 'window period'. However, while the test will produce antibody negative results during this six to 12 week window period, a person who has been infected with HIV may be even more infectious than at most other times during the progression of their HIV disease.

Anyone who thinks she may have been exposed to HIV should be advised to wait three months from the time of exposure before taking the test, but should be warned to ensure that her behaviour in the meantime is safe. If the individual has not repeated any risky practices during the maximum 12-week window period, and the HIV antibody test reveals a negative result, then she is not infected. The test may be repeated three months later, for added certainty, but it is very rare for the body to take longer than three months to produce enough antibodies for detection.

6.1 **To test or not to test?**

Reasons for taking the HIV antibody test vary greatly between individuals. The main purpose of the test is to confirm whether someone has HIV so they can then have access to the appropriate medical and care services. Testing for HIV is not a preventive measure; nor is knowing someone's HIV status necessary to prevent transmission. The HIV status of individuals is irrelevant if health and medical professionals are taking universal infection control precautions, and individuals adopt safer sex and safer drug-use practices.

The decision on whether to test should be seen in the context that HIV is a life-threatening condition. The vast majority of people who have tested HIV-positive report that the result was a life-changing experience. This is why HIV tests can only be performed with the full consent of the individual concerned.

Taking the test is something which should be considered very carefully. Many people take the test to confirm that they do not have HIV. It is important that anyone who takes the test considers in advance the possibility that the result may be positive, and is certain that they want to know. It is, however, always possible not to receive the result if someone changes their mind after giving blood for a test.

It is important that anyone who takes the test considers in advance the possibility that the result may be positive, and is certain that they want to know.

Some people think the test is an HIV prevention measure. It is not. There is no research evidence to show an absolute correlation between knowledge of HIV status and subsequent less risky behaviour. People make behavioural changes for far more complex reasons than knowing if they have HIV. Indeed, people who test HIV-negative may be more likely to engage in unsafe behaviour, despite the fact that this will jeopardise their HIV-negative status. For such people, the test could lead to a false, and harmful, sense of security. A negative HIV test result only gives information about HIV status at that point in time, and does not confer immunity to future infection. The need to consider safer sex and safer drugs use is universal: for people who know they are HIV-positive, those who test HIV-negative, and for those whose status is unknown.

6.1.1 Reasons to test

The primary reason for taking the HIV test is medical:
- *to establish the right diagnosis*. This could be in order to

understand properly why someone has health problems, or in the case of severe illness. The only circumstances in which doctors can order an HIV test without the person's consent is where they believe it is essential to establish the individual's HIV status so they can be given appropriate medical treatment

● *to monitor, and control, the development of an AIDS-related disorder.* For example, someone who is HIV-positive and asymptomatic should be monitored closely so that if the CD4 cell count drops below a certain level they can be advised to take prophylaxis against PCP. PCP used to be the prime cause of death for people with AIDS, but it is now seen less often and can usually be treated effectively

● *to encourage the individual to lead a more healthy lifestyle.* People who know they are HIV-positive can be helped to take greater care over their diet, exercise and general health

● *to allow early intervention.* Medical therapies have yet to be developed which, used during the asymptomatic period of HIV disease, can delay or prevent symptoms occurring. Researchers continue to explore treatments and new approaches.

Other reasons will be psycho-social. Among the more common reasons for people taking the HIV test are:

● *AIDS anxiety.* Some people experience heightened anxiety that they may have contracted HIV. It may put their minds at ease to know, one way or another

● *motivation.* People who know their HIV status may be motivated to adopt safer sex and drug using practices. Equally, however, a negative test may be seen as licence to continue to put themselves at risk

● *precautions.* Some people will want to take the test because of a relationship they are in, or intend to start. Knowing their HIV status will allow them to make choices about their sexual behaviour. If both test HIV-positive, or negative, they may choose not to have safer sex; or they may choose always to practise safer sex if they ever have sex outside their primary relationship

● *pregnancy.* Some women may want to know their partner's and their own HIV status before becoming pregnant. If a woman takes an HIV test for this purpose it is important that her male partner also considers being tested

- *lifestyle*. Knowledge of HIV status will allow the individual to reconsider how they organise their lives and their plans for the future. Neither an HIV nor an AIDS diagnosis is an instant death sentence, although it is often portrayed as such in the media. People with HIV and AIDS can continue to lead fulfilling lives for many years following diagnosis.

Finally, there may also be practical reasons:

- women and men involved in in vitro fertility programmes are required to take an HIV test, and the test must be negative
- all blood, semen and organ donors have to be HIV-negative
- some employers require employees to take an HIV test
- despite the fact that this is a breach of human rights, some countries require immigrants seeking residence to take an HIV test.

6.1.2 *Reasons not to test*

From a medical perspective, it is not essential to know if a healthy person has HIV. It can assist treatment if he or she develops a rare or serious AIDS-related illness. The HIV test gives no information about when or how a person was infected, nor when, or if, she will develop AIDS.

From a psycho-social perspective, people have widely differing reasons for not taking the test:

- *not wanting to know*. Some people prefer not to know unpleasant information, especially if there is little they can do to change or improve their situation
- *not considered necessary*. A person may be already practising safer sex and drug-use practices; she may fear that knowing she is HIV-negative may lessen her motivation
- *certainty that she is not infected*. In this situation it may be important to clarify the basis for that certainty, or to reinforce the importance of safer behaviour to protect from future infection. An individual may be sure she or he is not HIV-infected, but can they

be equally sure about their partner's status or sexual history, or that their partner is not having other sexual relationships?

A major reason not to take the HIV test is the stigma and discrimination attached to AIDS and HIV. People known to have HIV have been:

- evicted from their homes
- denied access to schools and further education
- sacked from their jobs and denied new employment
- abandoned by their families and rejected by their communities
- subjected to prejudice and hatred in day-to-day life
- denied entry to some countries (which can also affect their employment)
- refused insurance cover, and often refused mortgages.

Even people who have taken the test and tested negative can experience similar discrimination. Most life insurance applications (including those related to mortgages and financial investments) used to ask for information about whether people had been tested, and some companies considered that simply taking the test suggested that a person was at risk, and imposed a higher premium. The Association of British Insurers has, since July 1994, revised its guidelines to recommend that insurers ask only for details of positive testing and treatment for AIDS.

6.2 Where to test

If someone decides that she wants to know whether she has been infected with HIV, the next decision is where to take the test. The best place is usually the local genito-urinary medicine (GUM) or sexually transmitted disease (STD) clinic. One very important reason for choosing to go to a GUM (STD) clinic is that they are bound by law to keep all test results entirely confidential. This is a critical consideration for most people with HIV. Another benefit is that all patients taking the HIV test at a GUM clinic will receive both pre- and post-test counselling from a trained health adviser. Health advisers are highly skilled and experienced in dealing with HIV and other issues concerning sexuality. If a person tests positive the health adviser will be able to refer them on to specialist services available in the area. Health advisers can also help both HIV-negative and HIV-positive people develop strategies to avoid unsafe behaviour in the future, and can support the person in telling past and current partners if they wish.

HIV tests can also be obtained:

- at the GP surgery
- at the antenatal clinic
- in hospital
- in drug treatment and rehabilitation centres
- in prison
- at private test centres.

People donating blood will also be tested for HIV, but the blood transfusion service should not be used as a test centre.

Some people may not want to go to the GUM clinic, and may prefer to go for HIV testing to their GP, a drugs treatment service or other specialist centre. Clearly individual needs and circumstances should guide people's choices about where to be tested. However the quality of counselling and referral to specialist HIV services should be an important feature in choosing where to take the test. These factors tend to be overlooked, especially if a person is expecting a negative result, and it is important that health professionals raise these issues when offering advice to clients on taking an HIV test. Unskilled counselling may lead to people feeling coerced or under pressure to take the test, which itself may give rise to additional support needs.

GUM clinics are bound by law to keep all test results entirely confidential – a critical consideration for people with HIV.

6.3 HIV screening

Contrary to popular belief, there is no universal, individual screening programme for HIV in the UK. It is a widespread misconception that blood taken for other purposes is automatically also tested for HIV, and that individuals are told the result. The only way for a person to find out her HIV status is either specifically to request, or to accept the offer of a test. Similarly, as HIV is not a legally notifiable disease, there is no national policy for contact tracing, and people will not automatically be informed if a previous, or current, sexual partner has been tested HIV-positive.

Policies and practices for informing the sexual contacts of people tested HIV-positive vary from health district to health district: in some areas health advisers offer to help clients contact former and current partners (client referral); some GUM clinics will offer to contact former and current partners on behalf of the client (provider referral).[18]

Some people will be screened anonymously for HIV as part of an ongoing national survey of HIV prevalence being undertaken in selected STD and antenatal clinics and casualty departments throughout the UK. This screening programme has been introduced to provide epidemiological information about the prevalence of HIV, not to give individual test results. Under the scheme, blood which has been taken for another purpose is tested for HIV under strictly anonymous conditions: all identifying information except age, sex and sexual orientation (where known) of the patient is removed from the sample before the test is made, so the sample cannot be traced back to an individual. No-one whose blood is tested as part of the programme can therefore be told of their HIV status, and nor can anyone involved in the testing identify those testing HIV-positive.

Information should be prominently displayed and available in clinics and sites where the anonymous screening programme is operating, so that people may opt out if they choose. Health professionals should inform clients about the programme, and explain its purpose, that it is strictly anonymous, and that they will not be told the results, particularly if clients are thought unlikely to understand the written information available.

6.4 Testing infants

Similarly, there is no universal testing programme for all new-born infants. However, all babies born to mothers who are

HIV-positive will be tested for HIV unless the mother refuses consent. Doctors can only carry out the test without first obtaining the mother's consent if they believe the information is necessary to enable the child to receive appropriate treatment.

There are several reasons why doctors and the parents (or carers) of babies who may be HIV-infected will want to find out as early as possible if the baby is infected. These include:

● *wanting to know the real situation*. Less than 20 per cent of babies born to HIV-positive women are themselves HIV-infected,[12] and the chances that a baby will not be infected are therefore good. Not knowing if the baby is infected can cause great anxiety for the family

● *planning for the future*. Knowing whether the baby has HIV or not can be an important consideration in planning for the care of the child, particularly if fostering or adoption is being considered

● *access to appropriate medical and health care*. Most doctors will want to give HIV-infected babies prophylaxis against PCP, and the appropriate immunisations, and to ensure that they have good nutrition

● *monitoring the infant's immune system and overall development*. One in four babies infected with HIV develops AIDS or dies in the first year of life.[12] Since there is not yet a way of predicting the speed of the disease's progression, most doctors will want to monitor closely babies who are HIV-infected, in order to intervene swiftly if their health is failing

● *treatment*. Babies whose immune systems are failing may benefit from early treatment with anti-retrovirals, as well as prophylaxes. HIV-infected babies who become unwell will receive immediate treatment: for example, a baby with a fever will be started on intravenous antibiotics immediately.

Less than 20 per cent of babies born to HIV-positive women are themselves HIV-infected and the chances that a baby will not be infected are therefore good.

A few parents will not want to know early on whether their baby has HIV, or they may not want the baby to have blood tests. In these cases it is very important that the baby is treated as if she is HIV-infected, and receives close clinical monitoring, good nutrition, immunisations and, possibly, PCP prophylaxis.

However tests for HIV are not generally considered 100 per cent reliable until the baby is 18 months old. This is because all babies whose mothers are HIV-positive will have HIV antibodies from their mother's bloodstream, irrespective of whether they are HIV-infected themselves, and it is not possible accurately to distinguish the mother's antibodies from those of the baby for the first 18 months of an infant's life. Parents are likely to need much support during this period.

A definitive diagnosis of HIV-infection is secured in any of the following four ways:

- the presence of HIV-related symptoms or AIDS
- two positive viral tests (on separate samples, performed two weeks apart) showing the presence of p24 antigen or virus in peripheral blood
- one positive viral test with two abnormal immunological values (CD4:CD8 ratio, and immunoglobulin)
- persistent antibodies to HIV after 18 months.

There are three viral tests available and in use in the UK:
- the p24 antigen test, which shows if the protein of HIV is present in the blood
- the polymerase chain reaction (PCR) test, which looks for the genetic material in the virus and then magnifies it
- the HIV culture test, which grows the virus from a blood sample.

With all three tests, two positive results are required before a baby is diagnosed definitely HIV-infected.

Some 25 per cent of babies with HIV become ill or die in their first year of life,[12] and there may therefore be advantages in establishing an HIV diagnosis before 18 months of age, particularly if the mother is already known to be HIV-positive, or there is a strong likelihood that she has HIV (where, for example, the father is HIV-positive). A few specialist testing centres, with access to the sophisticated equipment and skills necessary, can now establish by four months if a baby born to an HIV-positive woman is infected. However the baby may have become infected at a later stage, during the actual birth process, or from breastfeeding; also it takes some time before HIV has replicated sufficiently to be detected. Negative tests prior to 18 months are therefore not generally accepted as definitive.

References

1   CETHV. An investigation into the principles of health visiting. London: CETHV, 1977.

2   McCarthy GA, Mercey D. The changing clinical features of HIV-1 infection in the UK. CDR Review 1994; 4,5: 53-58.

3   Gibb D, Walters S. Guidelines for management of children with HIV infection. Second edition. UK: Avert, 1993. A useful summary of current knowledge about paediatric AIDS can also be found in: National AIDS Manual (NAM) AIDS Treatment Update. Issue 13/14. November/December, 1993.

4   Gottlieb MS et al. Pneumocystis carinii pneumonia and mucosal candidiasis in previously healthy homosexual men. Evidence of a new acquired cellular immunodeficiency. The New England Journal of Medicine 1981; 305, 24: 1425-1431.

5   Montagnier L et al. Isolation of a T-lymphotropic retrovirus from patients at risk for acquired immune deficiency syndrome (AIDS). Science 1983; 220, 4599: 868-871.

6   Gallo RC et al. A pathogenic retrovirus (HTLV-III) linked to AIDS. New England Journal of Medicine 1984; 311, 20: 1292-1297.

7   This is an approximate figure based on back-projection techniques. See also: Day NE et al. Acquired immune deficiency syndrome in England and Wales to end 1993; projections using data to end September 1989. Communicable Diseases Report. Public Health Laboratory Service, January 1990.

8   Campbell P. Efficacy of female condom. The Lancet 1993; 341, 5: 1155.

9   Dunn DT et al. Risk of HIV-1 transmission through breastfeeding. The Lancet 1992; 340, 9: 585-588.

10   Chin J. Epidemiology: current and future dimensions of the HIV/AIDS pandemic in women and children. The Lancet 1990; 336: 221-224.

11   Newell M-L et al. Caesarean section and risk of vertical transmission of HIV-1 infection. The Lancet 1994; 343, 6: 1464-1467.

12   NAM. AIDS Treatment Update. Issue 13/14. November/December 1993.

13   Moffinson LM. Potential interventions for the prevention of perinatal transmission of HIV-1. Round table symposium; First National Conference on Human Retroviruses and Related Infections. Session 50. Washington DC. December 1993.

14   WHO. Special program on AIDS. Breastfeeding, breastmilk and the human immuno-deficiency virus (HIV). SPA/INF/87.8.

15   Department of Health. Guidance for clinical health care workers: protection against infection with HIV and hepatitis viruses. London: HMSO, 1990.

16   Oakley K. Making sense of universal precautions. Nursing Times 1994; 90, 27: 35-36.

17   Gill N et al. Occupational transmission of HIV: summary of published reports. Public Health Laboratory Service AIDS Unit, CDSC. Colindale, UK. May 1992.

18   See for example: Pattman R, Gould E. Partner notification for HIV infection in the UK: a look back on seven years' experience in Newcastle-upon-Tyne. Genitourinary Medicine 1993; 69: 94-97.

SECTION
2

HIV-positive clients

Clients who are known to be HIV-positive, or at high risk of being infected with HIV, will have many needs: for medical care, counselling and health advice, and for more general emotional and practical support and advice, to help them stay as well as possible for as long as possible.

A person with HIV or AIDS has to cope not only with a life-threatening diagnosis; she must also deal with the stigma attached to the condition, and the fact that it is infectious. With families, often all or most of the family members are likely to be infected, and there may be competing needs for care. If a baby is HIV-infected then her mother will also be HIV-positive. She will have to adjust not only to the child's diagnosis but also to her own HIV status and the possibility that other family members are infected. HIV-positive women who want to conceive, or who are pregnant, or have recently given birth may need a great deal of sensitive support from their health visitor, and up-to-date advice relevant to their special needs.

Many people with HIV/AIDS have acute social needs, which may pre-date their HIV diagnosis, and will be intensified by it. Many may have emotional issues which they may wish to address with health visitors. This section looks at the additional information health visitors, school nurses and practice nurses may need to underpin their professional skills when working with clients in such difficult circumstances.

7 Contraception

MANY WOMEN, ESPECIALLY after giving birth, will want information about contraception. They may be discussing this with their HIV specialist, GP or at the family planning clinic, but it is still useful to raise the issue. There has been very little research into contraceptives and HIV, with the exception of condoms and the femidom as protection against HIV transmission. These have a recognised significant failure rate and women who definitely do not want to conceive are advised to use another form of contraception in addition to condoms and lubricant.

In discussing contraception with women who are HIV-positive (or whose partners are HIV-positive) it is important to discuss their sexual lifestyle. Not all HIV-positive women, including those who are mothers, will necessarily be involved in sexual relationships with men, or with anyone, and some will have decided only to have non-penetrative sex. If both partners are HIV-positive they may choose to have unprotected sex, without a condom. They should be warned that it is still advisable to avoid acquiring STDs, and re-infection with HIV. The type and frequency of sexual activity, as well as whether future children are wanted, will also affect the choice of contraception.

Even if both partners are HIV-positive it is still advisable to use a condom to avoid re-infection with HIV and the risk of sexually transmitted diseases.

Some people will choose sterilisation or a vasectomy, especially if they already have children. However, it should not be assumed that this is the right course for all people with HIV and their partners. Using the diaphragm and spermicide, in addition to a condom, may be a good option for some women. Some partners may choose to use the two methods together only during fertile times of the menstrual cycle; others may decide not to have intercourse at all, even using condoms, during these times. Such forms of natural family planning may not be reliable for HIV-positive women, since many experience irregular menstrual cycles.

The coil, or IUD, increases the risk of pelvic infections, increases vaginal discharge and leads to heavier periods, all of which may increase the number of HIV-infected cells in the vagina and thus facilitate HIV transmission. The coil is therefore not recommended for a woman whose partner is HIV-negative, and in general is not recommended for HIV-positive women as it increases the existing high risk of pelvic inflammatory disease (PID).

There is little research into the oral contraceptive pill (OCP) and women with HIV.[1] There is some suggestion that the oral contraceptive pill is associated with risks to liver function, and that it may even suppress the immune system. It may not therefore be appropriate for current or former drug users who have liver damage. In addition the OCP may react with some HIV therapies (although this is rarely researched) and any antibiotic treatments (possibly including PCP prophylaxis) reduce the efficacy of this form of contraception. Some women may choose injectable contraception (which seems to have fewer side effects). This form of contraception can be more suitable for women who find it hard to remember to take the pill.[2]

Some people with HIV do not want to avoid conception. If they do want a child, or more children, it may be helpful to discuss the timing of a future pregnancy and how to reduce risks of HIV transmission between adults or to the baby.

8   Pregnancy

WOMEN WHO KNOW THEY are HIV-positive (or at high risk) may decide to become pregnant. There are as many reasons for HIV-positive women choosing to have a child as there are for any other woman. It will not be an easy decision for a woman with HIV, particularly when the general message, in the media and from society in general, tends to be prejudiced against such a choice. It is important for health professionals to respect the woman's choice and to try to understand her reasons.

8.1 Getting pregnant

The chances of an HIV-positive woman transmitting HIV to her baby are quite low: 14 per cent (one in seven) if she does not breastfeed.[3] The risk of transmission is less if the woman becomes pregnant when she is asymptomatic, her CD4 cell counts are high and her viral load is low. Specialist laboratories can assess this with tests for the p24 antigen (part of the HIV protein). Viral load is generally highest immediately after infection: usually during the first three months, which is before the antibody test gives a positive result. Viral load is also higher when a person is becoming unwell, and when she has other infections, including STDs.

Women whose male partners are HIV-positive may become pregnant or decide that they want to conceive. A woman wanting to conceive may choose to have unsafe sex only during her most fertile period and when her partner is likely to be less infectious. There is no easy or accurate test to detect this, but viral tests to detect whether p24 antigen is present may give some indication. Some doctors may be concerned about the ethical and legal

Women who know they are HIV-positive (or at high risk) may decide to become pregnant. It is important for health professionals to respect the woman's choice and to try to understand her reasons.

implications of carrying out viral tests for these purposes; they may worry that they will be held legally liable if the woman becomes infected. However, if the woman is determined to become pregnant such tests could help to reduce, but not eliminate, the risks. The woman needs to be counselled that by taking these measures she does risk acquiring HIV, and that even if she takes this route it will be important to practise safer sex after conception, and that it will, of course, take three months to find out whether she has become infected.

Some women feel the risks from natural conception are too high, and choose artificial insemination, either by anonymous donor or from, for example, a relative of her partner. This is already established practice where the male partner has a hereditary disease. All artificial insemination by donor (AID) services screen semen for HIV. If informal artificial insemination is being considered, the donor should be encouraged to take an HIV test at least three months after any risky behaviour.

In Italy there is a programme of artificial insemination for the partners of HIV-positive men. Seminal fluid from the HIV-positive man is treated by 'spinning' prior to insemination. This seems to render the fluid non-infectious, and women have conceived without sero-converting. This service is still experimental and is not currently available in the UK.

8.2 **During pregnancy**

All women, regardless of their known HIV status, should be encouraged to consider safer sex during pregnancy, since becoming HIV-infected during this time, and during breastfeeding, significantly increases the risks of transmission to the baby. All women who are pregnant should be encouraged to take care of their health, and this is just as important for women who are HIV-positive. Health promotion during this time will include good nutrition, exercise and relaxation.

With women who are HIV-positive, prophylaxes and anti-retroviral treatments should generally be continued, since these have not been shown to have teratogenic effects. Protecting the woman's health is important of itself, and may also lessen the risks of transmission to the fetus. This protection will also include protecting against re-infection with HIV and other STDs.

As both pregnancy and HIV alter the immune system, it used to be thought that pregnancy had a negative effect on HIV-positive women's health by speeding up disease. It is now known that this is only the case for women diagnosed with AIDS.[4]

Recent trials suggest that the risks of transmitting HIV to the fetus during pregnancy and delivery may be reduced by giving AZT.[5] This anti-retroviral therapy attempts to stop the virus from replicating by blocking the mechanism which transcribes RNA to DNA in the infected cell. Other experimental trials are looking at ways to reduce viral load, but there is currently no proven way to block HIV transmission inter- and intra-partum.

In the past, many women with HIV were counselled either not to conceive or to have terminations. Research has shown that abortion rates among women who know they have HIV are no different from general rates. In addition, there is strong anecdotal evidence to suggest that women who do have terminations (having, perhaps, felt coerced into doing so) often conceive again soon after.

It is becoming increasingly common for women to be offered HIV antibody testing at antenatal clinics, because of the risk of HIV transmission to the baby. Receiving a positive HIV test result is a traumatic, distressing experience, and all people with HIV need appropriate support and care. Women who have been diagnosed HIV-positive during pregnancy may have special needs. They have been diagnosed with a life-threatening condition at the same time as bringing a new life into the world. Childbirth is generally seen as a time of hope and new beginnings, and of making plans for the future. Women who are HIV-positive are likely to be anxious about whether their baby is infected, and may feel guilty at having exposed their child to HIV. They may neglect their

Women who are HIV-positive may feel guilty at having exposed their child to HIV. They may neglect their own medical and emotional needs.

own medical and emotional needs, and focus on the baby and other family members. Many women with HIV experience a sense of isolation and may benefit from meeting other HIV-positive women. The health visitor can help her client to identify her own health needs, and can provide information about local services and how to contact support groups.

8.3 **Delivery**

As discussed previously (see *Transmission*, p.20), HIV may be transmitted during delivery as well as pregnancy. Where possible, HIV-positive women should avoid invasive procedures, such as amniocentesis, forceps, vacuum extraction, and perhaps episiotomy. Prolonged exposure (over six hours) of the infant to ruptured membranes should also be avoided, as this is associated with a higher likelihood of transmission.[6,7] For some women delivery by caesarian section may be better, as research suggests this can reduce the risk of HIV transmission.[8]

For all new mothers, the period immediately following delivery can be stressful. Most new mothers want to know if their baby is healthy, but it may not be possible to tell if a baby is HIV-infected until she is at least four months old, and 18 months for a definitive diagnosis. This uncertainty about the HIV status of her baby may be distressing for an HIV-positive mother.

In addition, the tests to establish an early diagnosis involve taking a small amount of blood from the baby and, as there are several tests which have to be repeated, blood samples may have to be taken frequently. Some mothers find this upsetting. The mother may also find this time difficult if her family and loved ones are not aware of her status, if she has little support, or if she is a single parent. Sensitive support from her health visitor can be a major, positive contribution to helping a woman adjust to the many changes in her life.

> **Sensitive support from her health visitor may help a new mother who is HIV-positive adjust to the many changes in her life.**

9 Breastfeeding

IN THE PAST IT was not clear if HIV could be transmitted by breastfeeding. Unfortunately, we now know that there is a significant risk of HIV transmission by this route. The current advice is that HIV-positive women should not breastfeed if there are adequate alternatives, including a safe water supply. The risk of transmission from breastfeeding is now estimated at 14 per cent (one in seven), in addition to the risks of infection during pregnancy and delivery.[9] This risk rises to 30 per cent if the woman is infected while breastfeeding or in the last trimester of pregnancy (see *Transmission*, p.20).[3] The concentration of HIV seems to be particularly high in colostrum, and it has been suggested that it may be safer to breastfeed only from two weeks, or to pump breastmilk and then pasteurise it.[6] These do not seem to be realistic solutions.

In general, breastfeeding is important for a child's health: it confers immunity to infections, and it can be the source of important bonding between mother and child. In some cultures breastfeeding is the norm and women may find it hard to explain to relatives and friends if they choose not to breastfeed. This may be especially the case for some African women. Women in many third world countries lack access to clean water supplies for preparing formula feeds, and may not be able to afford to buy infant formulae. The World Health Organisation therefore recommends that in such circumstances breastfeeding is still the safer option.[10]

Some HIV-positive women (and women who have not taken an HIV test, but believe themselves to be at high risk of HIV) may feel under pressure to agree not to breastfeed. Some HIV-positive women have reported not daring to tell health professionals that they occasionally breastfeed. Breastfeeding should be the personal choice of all women. HIV-positive women should be helped to consider the extent of the risk,

HIV-positive women should not breastfeed, provided there are adequate alternatives, including a safe water supply.

and a non-judgemental approach from her health visitor can be an important source of information and support to a mother in adjusting to her situation and providing the best care for her child.

The newborn infant should not be put to the breast if the mother has decided not to breastfeed.

10 Children born to HIV-positive women

IN THE UK THERE have, as yet, been relatively few births to HIV-positive women; most of these have been in London and Edinburgh. Most doctors and other health professionals in the UK therefore have little experience in dealing with paediatric HIV disease. Some hospitals and health services have developed specialist services: for example, Great Ormond Street Hospital in London and City Hospital, Edinburgh, both of which operate a shared-care programme for these children.[11]

As previously explained, all babies born to HIV-positive women will have HIV antibodies from their mother's bloodstream, irrespective of whether they are HIV-infected themselves (see

Testing Infants, p.48). Only a minority of babies born to HIV-positive women will themselves be infected, but until a definitive diagnosis is made most doctors will want to monitor all these babies closely, and will probably treat them as if they are infected.

Uninfected babies born to HIV-infected women may have special needs unrelated to any medical condition. Many of these children will ultimately be orphaned, and their long-term care will need to be carefully planned. If other members of the family are HIV-positive, the child may be neglected due to competing care needs. Conversely the child may become the focus of extreme attention, as the family's 'survivor'.

10.1 **Signs and symptoms**

The signs and symptoms associated with HIV disease in both adults and children are often similar to those of other, more common and less severe conditions. Health visitors should therefore be extremely cautious about 'diagnosing' children whose parents are known, or suspected, to be HIV-positive. In general, the parents should be encouraged to take the child to see the GP if she is unwell or failing to thrive.

A particularly difficult feature of HIV-infected babies is that 25 per cent develop AIDS or die in the first year of life; often before there is a definitive diagnosis of their HIV-infection.[12] This is largely why there is so much emphasis on the need for tests which can accurately diagnose HIV as early as possible, so that babies can receive appropriate treatment. The most serious condition these babies can develop is PCP (pneumocystis carinii pneumonia). Babies in whom the disease progresses more rapidly may develop conditions other than PCP (and not all develop PCP), but this is the condition of principle concern.

As with adults, PCP can occur at any time, but mainly occurs in the first three to six months of the infant's life. Many of the babies who develop it at this time will not survive. Prophylaxis exists which may help to prevent PCP: usually trimethoprim-sulfamethoxasole (known as Septrin or Bactrim). There are no agreed guidelines about giving this, and HIV-positive infants may be given PCP prophylaxis before a definitive diagnosis is secured, once HIV infection is established, or only if their CD4 cells fall below safe levels. Children who do not receive PCP prophylaxis need to be monitored particularly carefully, and should be seen regularly by the paediatrician.

Parents and carers should be alert for early symptoms of PCP and contact a doctor immediately if the child has:

- dry, persistent cough
- shortness of breath or difficulty in breathing
- high fever (with no other cause).

Children who do not develop AIDS in their first year have a similar progression of HIV to adults. Forty per cent of children born with HIV will have developed AIDS by the age of four. Thereafter, each year approximately one in 14 of children who are still well have gone on to develop AIDS. The length of time a child survives after an AIDS diagnosis varies. Some 30 per cent of children are still alive three years after being diagnosed with AIDS. In total, 75 per cent of children born infected with HIV have lived to the age of five, and 50 per cent have survived to celebrate their ninth birthday.[12]

> **Parents and carers should be alert for early symptoms of PCP and contact a doctor immediately.**

In addition to PCP, infants with HIV may be subject to other opportunistic and bacterial infections, and HIV itself causes direct damage, in particular to the brain and lungs. Many infants, especially the 75 per cent who do not become ill in the first year of life, have only very general symptoms at first. These include swelling of the liver or spleen (hepato/splenomegaly), swollen lymph glands in the neck, underarm and groin (generalised lymphadenopathy), diarrhoea, fever (with no other causes), and failure to thrive. These are all conditions that can also occur in children who do not have HIV, and it may be difficult for a doctor to tell if the symptoms are linked to HIV infection, especially if there is no definite diagnosis of the infant's HIV status.

Children with HIV may also develop:

- parotitis (swollen parotid glands, similar in appearance

to severe mumps)

● lymphocytic interstitial pneumonitis (a lung problem leading to cough, shortness of breath and pneumonias)

● thrombocytopenia (low platelets, which may cause bruising on the skin and, in severe cases, internal bleeding)

● candida (thrush, either in the mouth and/or nappy rash, which tends to be persistent in children with HIV and to respond poorly to treatment).

In addition, infants with HIV are more vulnerable to serious and recurring infections from common childhood illnesses. These can cause pneumonia, meningitis and infections of the blood, bone and skin. Chicken pox and other herpes infections may cause severe illness in children infected with HIV, and measles can be fatal.

10.2 **Immunisations**

In order to prevent childhood illnesses, it is important that children with HIV are immunised. Immunisations are generally effective in children who do not have symptoms, but they are less effective if the child is symptomatic or has AIDS. Immunisations should be given at the normal time for diphtheria, tetanus, pertussis (DPT); hib; polio; measles, mumps and rubella (MMR); diphtheria, tetanus and polio. Particular points to note are:

● zoster, or measles immunoglobulin should be given to a symptomatic HIV-positive child (of any age) who is in contact with chicken pox or measles, as this will help to prevent the illness or make it less severe. It is important to tell the doctor if any HIV-positive child has been exposed to these illnesses

● children with HIV may be offered flu vaccination as a preventive measure in epidemics, or at the beginning of winter, according to individual circumstances and need

● hepatitis B vaccine will be given to babies whose mother is hepatitis B positive

● live polio vaccine may be given to an HIV-positive

child unless a parent or carer is also HIV-positive, in which case inactive polio may be given instead, to avoid possible infection of other immuno-compromised family members

● BCG vaccine against tuberculosis should not be given to children known to be HIV-infected, or those born to an HIV-positive mother.

10.3 Management of children with HIV

Where a child is known to be HIV-positive or HIV-infected, or her parents are receiving HIV services, teams of health professionals including HIV specialists will be monitoring the child's health. Health visitors can be an important part of this team, offering support and care which complements the skills and disciplines of other professionals. These multi-disciplinary teams may be small, or may include a wide range of professionals, including an adult HIV specialist, paediatri-

Families with HIV need as much support as any other family with the everyday challenges of parenting and child-rearing.

cian, GP, psychologist, dietician, nurse specialist, social worker, counsellors, and voluntary carers such as a 'buddy'.

Health visitors are trusted health professionals, who have built a relationship with the family at home. The support they may be able to offer will be different from that provided by the many professionals with a more medical focus. HIV disease does have acute phases, but in most cases there are extended periods when both children and adults with HIV are well. Families with HIV need as much support as any other family with the everyday chal-lenges of parenting and child-rearing, including dealing with normal childhood diseases.

Nutritional advice is important. All people with HIV should be encouraged to have a healthy, balanced diet, high in calories and protein. This is particularly important for children who are vulnerable to failure to thrive.

It can be a great comfort and support to parents to have

help with their child's general development, and care which is not always focused on HIV and AIDS. Indeed, some families may feel 'taken over' by their HIV diagnosis, and that being able to live a 'normal life' gives them more impetus to cope and survive. Since most children born to HIV-positive women do not develop AIDS, and many who are HIV-infected survive to school age, these children need just as much 'normal' attention as they do specialist HIV-focused care.

11   HIV and the school-age child

As previously stated, 75 per cent of the children born infected with HIV have survived to the age of five.[12] Children with HIV and AIDS are currently attending schools, and will do so in increasing numbers as incidence spreads and survival rates improve. Other children have been infected by HIV-contaminated blood products, and from sharing needles and unprotected sex. The school will not always know if there are HIV-positive children among its pupils. Many families may be wary of telling the school, since some children with HIV have been harassed and discriminated against in schools, because of the irrational fears of other parents.

Health visitors and school nurses may be able to support the family in making decisions about whether to tell the school and whom to tell. They will, for example, know if the school has a policy on HIV, and what the general attitude is. If the health visitor or school nurse takes on such a role it is important that she protects her clients' confidentiality. It is for the family to decide if they want other health professionals or school staff to know. Health visitors and school nurses should follow the 'need to know' principle in their decisions about whether and which colleagues to inform: that is, on the basis of their own professional judgement that it is in the best interests of the child, the family, and others who might be at risk (see *Confidentiality*, p.88). No-one should be told without the family's consent. The family may decide they wish their health visitor to inform the school nurse when their child starts school. This will enable the school nurse to work closely with the health visitor to ensure the child's special needs continue to be met.

It is for the family to decide if they want other health professionals or school staff to know their child's HIV status.

With regard to general good practice, the school nurse has an important role in ensuring that the school provides a supportive environment for all children, regardless of HIV status. She can help in the development of whole-school policies on HIV/AIDS: for example, by ensuring that good standards of hygiene and infection control are in place throughout the school, and by monitoring that these are adhered to. This will reduce the risk of transmission of all infectious diseases, and ensure that if a child is known to have HIV precautions are already in place to avoid risk to other children or to school staff.

Where a school is informed that a child has HIV infection, the family or carers will want to know which of the school staff have been told, and should be reassured that the information will be kept confidential.

The school will probably encourage the parents to tell the school nurse. Knowing a child's HIV status will enable the school nurse to give any support and special care the child needs, and provide appropriate care if the child is unwell. The school nurse will also be aware of any serious childhood illnesses occurring among the school population, and should ensure teaching staff keep her informed. Chicken pox and measles pose a particular threat to an HIV-infected child, and the school nurse should inform the parents or carers if there is a risk that a child with HIV has been exposed to these conditions.

In addition to medical support, children with HIV may need a great deal of personal support. Some children will not know that they have HIV, and may be distressed that they are often unwell, or that they have to visit the doctor or hospital so frequently. Some will have parents and siblings who are unwell or who have died because of HIV/AIDS; they may be living with foster carers, adopted parents or their extended family; they may need special help to cope with their grief and these major life changes. This may also be the case with the many children who are personally affected by HIV/AIDS although not themselves infected.

The school nurse has an important role in ensuring that the school provides a supportive environment for all children, regardless of their HIV status.

Most children at school, especially in secondary schools, receive sex education and education about HIV/AIDS. Often the school nurse will have a role in this [see Section three below]. HIV-positive school-age children will also need to learn about HIV transmission, especially as they reach adolescence. Most HIV-positive adolescents will have been told about their HIV status, but not all will know and this can pose special problems for school nurses and health visitors involved with their care.

Children who are closely affected by HIV (whether or not they have HIV themselves) may find school lessons which address HIV/AIDS issues distressing. School nurses who are aware of their home and family situation may be able to offer individual support without compromising these children's confidentiality.

12 Families living with HIV

INCREASINGLY, HIV IS A family disease. The dynamics of HIV infection mean that several members of the same family may be HIV-positive. Where this is not the case and only one member is infected, the family as a unit may still be seriously affected and may have many concerns centred on HIV/AIDS.

The term 'family' is used here in the broadest sense; the family unit may take many forms other than the traditional unit of a man and woman and their children. They may be extended families, with other relatives providing care; they may be 'traditional' families, single-parent families, or families where the primary relationships are between more than two adults. For example, many gay and bisexual men have children and may maintain a close relationship with them even if they do not live with the child's mother; two women may share parental responsibility for a child, while the biological father is also involved; there may be other adults external to the primary parent-child unit who have a central, recognised role in a child's life.

Families will be more confident and willing to explain their structures and their needs to health visitors and school nurses if they feel secure that the health professional is open to the diversity of relationships which can exist.

Families living with HIV have many concerns beyond purely medical matters. As previously stated, there will often be several HIV specialists involved in their care, and communication and co-operation between these professionals is important. This will both ensure that the family's range of health, medical and social care needs are addressed, and that **The health visitor will be able to help the family identify their principle needs, and balance these with the needs of the child.** professionals do not duplicate or compete with their services. It can often happen that one aspect of a family's needs is met with high quality specialist care but the needs of the family unit as a whole are not addressed. When a child is HIV-infected, adults may find that they and the professionals focus a great deal of attention on her needs, but that the needs of the adult(s) are neglected. Where the child is not infected, the HIV-positive adults' needs for attention and support may at times conflict with the demands of parenting or the needs of the child. The health visitor will be able to help the family identify their principle needs, and balance these with the needs of the child. Often a family's needs will not be directly, or obviously related to their HIV status.

12.1 **Health promotion**

Families living with HIV have the same health promotion needs and opportunities as those where no family member is HIV-infected. In addition to these needs, they will have special needs with regard to healthy living and nutrition, infection control and family planning.

People with HIV need 'secondary prevention' intervention: that is, health advice and education to avoid developing or exacerbating HIV symptoms, or precipitating the development of AIDS. Some of these interventions will be medical, such as PCP prophylaxis; others will centre on healthy lifestyle.

Like anyone else, people with HIV should be encouraged to take exercise. The nature of the exercise will depend on individual preference and strength, but should not stop if a person becomes ill since it is important to guard against muscle-wastage. Many people with HIV experience stress, and can be encouraged to learn and practise stress management techniques. Support groups can be helpful, including those for stress management and relaxation such as meditation or yoga classes.

Good nutrition is always important for people with serious health conditions, and is of particular importance with HIV disease, in which wasting, weight loss, diarrhoea and loss of appetite are common. There are no special guidelines, but people should be encouraged to have a balanced diet, high in calories and protein. Fresh fruits and vegetables provide vitamins and minerals, and these may be supplemented by multi-vitamins or any specific vitamins which are deficient. People who have lost their appetite or who are nauseous should be encouraged to eat what they feel like, to keep their weight up; people with diarrhoea should be encouraged to drink plenty of liquids.

Good hygiene in food preparation is important, and hands should be washed before eating or preparing food. People with HIV are especially vulnerable to bacteria such as salmonella, and great care should be taken with the storage and preparation of eggs and chicken. Similarly, raw meats should be avoided, because of the possible risks of toxoplasmosis. Water should be boiled if there is any concern about its quality. Care should be taken with handling pets, as diseases can be transmitted from animal faeces.

Some HIV-positive parents may be anxious that they will infect their babies or other children. The only known route of infection after birth is breastfeeding, and parents can be reassured that it is perfectly safe to care for and hug, kiss and cuddle their children as normal. Good hygiene should be practised (see also *Infection control*, p.34). This will include not sharing toothbrushes (and razors for adults), as there is a slight possibility that HIV-infected blood could be transmitted this way. However there have been numerous studies confirming that everyday living with people with HIV poses no risk of transmission. There is absolutely no risk of infection from using the same cutlery and crockery or bathroom facilities, or from general nursing of people with HIV.

Parents should be reassured that it is perfectly safe to care for, hug, kiss and cuddle their child as normal.

Finally, adults and adolescents in families with HIV may need information about sexual health. The majority of adults with HIV will have received a great deal of information and advice about safer sex and safer drugs use, where this is an issue. However they may still have questions and concerns which they want to discuss with the health visitor. Women with HIV can feel that they are no longer seen as sexual beings, and are often wrongly assumed to be celibate.

Like all children, children with and affected by HIV need sex education appropriate to their age and development. Health visitors and school nurses can help families to talk to their children about sexual issues, including discussing questions about HIV.

12.2 Emotional issues

Every individual affected or concerned about HIV will have a different, individual emotional response. Health visitors and school nurses are experienced in listening to and supporting their clients, and these skills will be essential in working with families affected by HIV. It will be difficult for any adult or child to adjust to a positive diagnosis of HIV or AIDS, and it may take a long time. For many people this will be an extremely painful and distressing period, and they will need a lot of support. They may need several people to listen, perhaps many times over, to their concerns, or they may want to have some 'AIDS-free' time when they can concentrate on the other parts of their lives. For some people, receiving a positive diagnosis can be a relief, especially if they have been anxious about HIV for a long time.

There is no right way to deal with a diagnosis; every individual will react differently. Some people may go through 'stages' of grief: the process of denial, anger, bargaining and depression leading to acceptance, as identified by Elizabeth Kubler-Ross.[13] Other people's response will be less linear. Someone may seem to have 'dealt' with an HIV diagnosis, but then react very strongly when she or her child develops a symptom.

Health visitors and school nurses are experienced in listening to and supporting their clients, and these skills will be essential in working with families affected by HIV.

Adults can find it extremely difficult to tell a child that she, or someone she loves, has HIV or AIDS. They may be concerned about the child's ability to understand the information; worry that she will not be able to keep the information confidential, and that she (or the family) will suffer if other people know, or fear the strength of the child's emotional response if she is told. But children will often be aware that something is wrong, even if they have not been told or do not understand what the problem is. Children can be more upset by an awareness that adults are keeping something hidden from them, and worry that the hidden problem is their fault. Adults may need a lot of support in choosing when and how to tell a child about their own or a loved one's HIV status.

It can be extremely hard to predict how serious an HIV or AIDS-related illness will be, and what its outcome will be. This uncertainty, and the difficulty in predicting which of many different courses the disease may take, can be another major source of family stress. Despite the widely-held view that diagnosis of AIDS is an immediate 'death sentence', many people with AIDS continue full lives, and come through several episodes of serious illness.

It can be very difficult for families to plan for the future. It may seem unduly pessimistic and negative when someone is well to discuss making arrangements for after their death; during periods of illness there will be more pressing, immediate concerns. But planning for the future is important when there are children involved, and parents who have HIV or AIDS will need to consider who will take care of the children if they become seriously ill or die. Social workers will help with this planning, and specialist help is available. One such source of help and information is the Barnardo's 'Positive Options' scheme (see *Resources*, p.100) but there are others, often attached to hospitals with specialist AIDS and HIV services, run by hospices, or organised by AIDS groups. Parents may want to make 'memory stores': books or boxes with mementoes about themselves and their children, for the children to have as they grow up. Facing the fact that they may not survive to see their children

Planning for the future is important when there are children involved. Parents with HIV or AIDS will need to consider who will take care of the children if they become seriously ill or die.

grow to adulthood can be extremely distressing. These long-term issues are often painful and difficult and the family may want to discuss them with several people, especially professionals and workers who know them well or have been involved with them over a long period of time.

Families will need support when a member of the family dies of AIDS, as they would with a family death from any other cause. In the case of a death from AIDS, this may also be a stark reminder that other family members are likely to die, or bring back memories of those who have already died of AIDS or other causes. Children will need help to understand what has happened, and to express their emotions. This may be especially difficult if, say, a surviving parent is worried about having developed AIDS herself, or has concerns about the child's health.

Again, this is one of the particular features of AIDS: where there is multiple HIV infection, there is also multiple grief and mourning.

References

1   Johnson MA, Johnstone FD (eds). HIV infection in women. London: Churchill Livingstone, 1993.

2   See also: Bury J. Pregnancy, heterosexual transmission and contraception. In Bury J et al. Working with women and AIDS: medical, social and counselling issues. London: Routledge, 1992.

3   Newell M-L et al. European collaborative study. Risk factors for mother-to-child transmission of HIV-1. The Lancet 1992; 339, 8800: 1007-1012.

4   Schoenbaum EE et al. The impact of pregnancy on HIV-related disease. In Hudson C, Sharp F (eds). AIDS and obstetrics and gynaecology. London: Royal College of Obstetricians and Gynaecologists, 1988.

5   NIAID. Important therapeutic information on the benefit of Zidovudine for the prevention of the transmission of HIV from mother to infant. Preliminary results of trial ACTG 076. Clinical Alert. 22 February, 1994.

6   NAM. AIDS Treatment Update. Issue 13/14. November/December 1993.

7   Moffinson LM. Potential interventions for the prevention of perinatal transmission of HIV-1. Round table symposium. First National Conference on Human Retroviruses and Related Infections. Washington DC. Session 50. 12-16 December, 1993.

8   Newell M-L et al. Caesarian section and risk of vertical transmission of HIV-1 infection. The Lancet 1994; 343, 6: 1464-1467.

9   Dunn DT et al. Risk of HIV-1 transmission through breastfeeding. The Lancet 1992; 340: 585-588.

10   WHO. Breastfeeding, breastmilk and the human immunodeficiency virus. Special program on AIDS. Statement SPA/INF/87.8.

11   Gibb D, Walters S. Guidelines for management of children with HIV infection. Second edition. UK: Avert, 1993.

12   Gibb D, Newell M-L. HIV infection in children. Archives of Diseases in Childhood 1992; 67: 138-141.

13   Kubler-Ross E. On death and dying. London: Tavistock Publications, 1969.

SECTION 3

HIV prevention and sex education

Health visitors and school nurses have a major contribution to make to the fight against AIDS and HIV. Very few health visitors and school nurses will currently be working with families who are personally affected by HIV and AIDS. The aim must be to keep it this way. Despite years of research into the disease and its treatment, prevention remains the only 'cure'. This should be a primary focus for health visitor, school nurse and practice nurse interventions in health promotion and sex education.

13   Adults and young people

HEALTH VISITORS, SCHOOL nurses and practice nurses have a vital role to play in HIV prevention with the adult population and young people. As trusted professionals who can offer health advice in the home, and in the context of routine contacts with clients, health visitors have unique access and opportunity to educate a large number of sexually-active adults, and to offer them the opportunity to explore any HIV risks they may face and develop strategies for reducing these risks. Health visitors and school nurses can also help parents talk to their children about sex, so that basic principles, such as body-awareness, are established when children are still very young. Practice nurses also have many opportunities to introduce sexual health advice in the context of 'well-person' clinic sessions and other routine contacts with patients on the practice register.

13.1 Raising the issues

Sex education should be a continuous process; part of every child's learning and personal development. Sexual health advice also needs to be reinforced as the child grows older, and similarly reassessed with adults as their circumstances change.

After the birth of a new baby it is natural to reconsider contraceptive measures and family planning. This is something which most health visitors will discuss with their clients. Many women may also want to discuss other sexual health issues with health visitors. These may typically include such issues as how soon after the delivery they can have intercourse, what are the implications of episiotomy, and how to cope with having less desire or energy for sex. Some may also have questions about HIV and AIDS, especially if they were tested for HIV at the antenatal clinic.

Having a child is a major life event, and can be a time when women re-evaluate many aspects of their life. Many of us find it difficult to discuss our sex lives. It is not something we are generally encouraged to do, and we can find it awkward and embarrassing. However all these new mothers have had sex, and most will continue to do so, and therefore it is entirely appropriate to discuss and address any concerns they may have.

It is rare that we have an opportunity to discuss sexual health, and with a health professional who knows us and has an ongoing relationship with us in a non-medical context. This is a service health visitors can uniquely provide.

A healthy sex life is an essential component of overall health and well-being. It is rare that we have an opportunity to discuss sexual health, and with a health professional who knows us and has an ongoing relationship with us in a non-medical context. Enabling clients to explore their concerns and needs in this area is thus an important service that health visitors can uniquely provide.

Many health visitors will routinely raise these issues, asking women about sex or contraception. Others will wait until the client asks questions. For many women it may be easier if the health visitor begins the discussion about sex, as this can make it seem a more acceptable topic for discussion.

Most people will find it easiest to discuss sex if the professional is comfortable with the subject matter and the language, and if she has a non-judgemental approach. How these issues are raised will depend on the client: for example, some will relate better to a humorous approach which breaks the ice; others will prefer a more medical or technical approach, and some may be distressed by the subject and need help with this. What is important is to offer women the opportunity - preferably several opportunities - to talk about the whole range of sexual issues. This might include:

- her current sexual relationships
- contraceptive needs
- how she feels about sex
- different sexual activities
- sexually-transmitted diseases
- the facts about HIV transmission and safer sex.

Sexual health needs are best addressed holistically, in the individual's total life context. This is true also for AIDS and HIV. Addressing HIV/AIDS in isolation will rarely be helpful; HIV/AIDS is one factor in the whole continuum of sexuality and sexual health. A woman may fully understand the facts about HIV, perceive herself to be at high risk, but feel unable to act on this information because of other factors, such as lack of control over her sexual choices and involvements. Many women will see HIV/AIDS as nothing to do with them, and health visitors may be reluctant to raise the subject with clients, for fear of upsetting them by an apparent suggestion that either they or their partner may be unfaithful, or that the relationship is unstable, or that they may be using drugs. For all these reasons, HIV/AIDS should not be raised abruptly, out of the context of sexual health in general.

13.2 Risk assessment

Some groups of people have suffered disproportionately from the impact of AIDS, and this is relevant to the assessment of risk at an individual level. For 100 per cent of the population to adopt safer sex practices 100 per cent of the time would be the most effective way to prevent further spread of HIV, but this is hardly a realistic goal. Risk assessment can, at the very least, enable people to identify and make decisions on the basis of their likely vulnerability to HIV, although this is by no means foolproof.

Risk assessment involves analysing the individual's potential for, or likelihood of contracting or having contracted HIV.

Women need to know the extent to which the men with whom they have had unprotected sex (or shared drug-injecting equipment) were vulnerable to having acquired HIV. When discussing sexual histories or previous drug use, it is relevant to remember that HIV only became established in the UK around 1987, so it is unlikely that anyone would have become infected through unprotected sex or sharing drug-use equipment before that.

The overwhelming majority of HIV-positive women have been infected by unprotected anal or vaginal sex with HIV-positive men, or by sharing injecting equipment with HIV-positive women and/or men. A few have been infected by contaminated blood transfusions.

It is easy enough for women to assess if they have a risk of contracting HIV from shared injecting equipment (although it may not be easy for them to reveal this risk). Women need to understand that this is an extremely efficient route of HIV transmission, and that injecting equipment should not be shared with anyone, not even sexual partners.

It is more difficult in particular for women to assess their risk of infection from sex. HIV/AIDS statistics show that a significant number of women are categorised as being infected through 'no known risk'; this is presumably because the women did not know if their partner had HIV, or if he had engaged in risk behaviours, and therefore contracted the virus unknowingly.

The majority of HIV-positive men have been infected by unprotected anal sex with HIV-positive men, or by sharing injecting equipment with HIV-positive women and/or men. These are all issues which a man may be unwilling to disclose to others. A number of men have been infected by contaminated blood products or transfusions. Again, whether they disclose this to a prospective sexual partner is usually a matter of personal choice and responsibility. As previously explained, HIV/AIDS is not an officially notifiable disease.

Some women will know that their partner is from a country where HIV prevalence is high (for example, in central Africa), or has haemophilia, injects drugs or is bisexual, and unless they are certain that he is HIV-negative, they should be aware that at present he has a higher than average vulnerability to HIV. However, sex between men and drug use are both highly stigmatised behaviours and are frequently concealed, despite the fact that significant numbers of people engage in them. Men may thus be frightened to reveal risk behaviours to their sexual partners, and this makes it extremely difficult for women to make accurate assessments of their personal risk.

Women who have multiple sexual partners have been categorised as being at high risk of acquiring HIV. Having unprotected sex with several men clearly involves a greater vulnerability to HIV than unprotected sex with one man, because there is a higher statistical risk of having sex with a man with HIV. However, it is not the number of partners which is significant to the transmission of HIV; it is the safety of the sexual behaviour. Unprotected sex with one HIV-positive man is far more risky than protected sex with several men. Some women have multiple partners for pleasure, and others may do so for practical or financial reasons. Women who work in the commercial sex industry have a high level of awareness of HIV, and most prostitutes practise safer sex. Women who are only occasionally involved in exchanging sex for money or goods may have less knowledge and motivation always to use condoms. If a client is known to be involved in selling sex, however infrequently, it will be important to ensure that she is aware of the risks, knows the basic principles of safer sex, and has access to free condoms and lubricant.

However, contrary to popular prejudice perhaps, the majority of HIV-positive women infected through sex became infected in long-term relationships. It can be extremely distressing for a woman even to consider that her partner may be exposing her to risk of HIV infection. It can cause great stress, and easily translate into relationship problems. There is an important balance to be struck between ensuring that a client understands about HIV and has the opportunity to explore any risks, and not scaring her unduly. Health visitors are in the ideal position of having a routine, ongoing, one-to-one relationship with their clients, and are often

It is not the number of partners which is significant to the transmission of HIV; it is the safety of sexual behaviour.

involved with a family over a number of years – or even genera-
tions. This contact and knowledge of family history and context
can help in assessing a client's risk and needs. However, it is important not to allow assumptions about risk to prevent opportunities
for the client to discuss her concerns.

Clients who assess they may have been at risk, or need to
avoid risk in a current relationship, will need information about
safer sex and safer drug use. Advice alone may not be sufficient;
often clients need practical information – for example, where to get
free condoms – and specific personal support in developing skills. It
can be especially difficult for a woman to ask for, or insist on, safer
sex. This will be even harder if safer sexual practices are introduced
into an existing relationship. The suggestion is highly loaded with
implications about sexual fidelity, or lifestyle.

Clients might want to try out various ways of raising the
subject with their partner, and the health visitor can be a useful
sounding board for this. There are many different ways for a
woman to raise the issue of safer sex with her partner: discussing
safer sex and HIV in general; asserting her needs during sex; insti-
gating condom use, or using humour to persuade.

Some clients may decide that they want to know if they
are HIV-infected. The section on HIV testing (p.42) gives information on the procedures and the issues which need to be considered before taking the test. If a client decides to take a test, it may
help her to discuss the issues with her health visitor (or, if taking the
test through her GP, the practice nurse), who can help her to think
through why she wants to take the test, how she will react if she is
HIV-positive, and what changes either result will make to her
current and future behaviour. If the client is in a sexual relationship, it may be a good idea for both partners to discuss her decision
to take the test, and perhaps both be tested together.

The client should be advised not to tell too many people if
she is taking the test, or to tell only those people whom she would
inform if the result is positive and she does prove to have
HIV/AIDS. Clients should also be encouraged to take the test
where they will receive the best pre- and post-test counselling,
such as the GUM clinic.

14   School-age children

SCHOOL NURSES ARE increasingly involved in the general health promotion programmes which both primary and secondary schools are now developing. The best of these programmes will include sex education and information about HIV/AIDS and its prevention. The skills and knowledge of the school nurse can offer a great deal to the proper development of such work.

14.1   The framework

National legislation on sex education and government policies on the teaching about HIV/AIDS in schools are subject to constant review and revision. The most recent is the Education Act 1993, and its accompanying guidance.[1] The Sex Education Forum is a useful source of information and updating on current legislation and policy, and can also provide expert advice, information, and training. Another useful resource is the Family Planning Association (see *Resources* for details of how to contact both these organisations), which also provides useful teaching, training and sex education materials.

Under the Education Act 1993 and accompanying guidance, sex education may be provided in local authority primary schools, and is compulsory in local authority secondary schools, although parents may withdraw their child from these classes. However teaching about AIDS and HIV may only be included in the sex education programme; it may not form part of the science curriculum, for example. Independent and grant-maintained schools are expected to follow these guidelines, although they are not legally obliged to do so.

Every school is expected to have an agreed policy on sex education, which is decided by the school's governing body, and parents must be informed of this policy. A school's sex education policy is likely to be guided by advice from the local education authority, and sometimes the district health authority, within the framework of national government guidelines. These policies may be extremely detailed, or simply a brief statement of principle.

The law and national policy and guidelines recognise in general that sex education is important for young people, but also emphasise the importance of parental involvement and a moral framework of 'family values'. The provision of sex education in schools is poorly understood by many people; balanced and responsible sex education can easily be misrepresented by the popular press as morally shocking, permissive, or even sexually sala-cious. This can make for a highly pressurised environment for the teaching and health staff involved.

There are many persuasive arguments to support the pro-vision of comprehensive sex education in schools. Sex education is wanted, needed and contributes to the health and well-being of young people. There is good evidence to show that sex education enhances the health of young people, both in general terms and through the prevention of disease and unwanted pregnancy. Research confirms that good sex education in school encour-ages more responsible sexual behaviour among children and young people, and that teaching about AIDS and sex education does not result in earlier or increased sexual activity, and may in fact may result in increased uptake of safer sex practices.[2]

Sex education is wanted, needed and contributes to the health and well-being of young people.

Clearly children and adolescents want and need informa-tion about sex and sexuality; it is fundamental to their personal development and the process of growing up. Children are naturally curious about their bodies, and sexual development is an impor-tant, and natural, part of becoming an adult. Lack of sexual know-ledge and understanding, sexual ignorance and suppression of sexual feelings can cause great harm. It has even been suggested that not providing effective sex education, or allowing parents to dictate whether their child attends sex education classes, is in breach of the Children's Act 1989 and United Nations human rights conventions, which uphold the principles that children's interest are paramount, and that their rights to information, knowledge and education should be respected.[3]

The level of myth and misinformation surrounding sex education in schools means that school nurses will find it useful and important to develop alliances with each other, and with other professionals such as teaching staff, health promotion officers and people working in voluntary sector AIDS organisations. This can provide an important source of support to the individual school nurse, who may be otherwise working in professional isolation. It will also help raise the profile and enhance general understanding of the importance and value of sex education.

14.2 **The approach**

Sex education which focuses only on the biological or medical dimensions of sex, such as reproduction and STDs, is rarely successful in enhancing children's positive understanding about sexual health. The ways in which we develop our attitudes to sex, decide on behaviour and contexts for sexual expression, and respond to sexual health concerns are complex. Effective sex education not only provides information, but also offers pupils opportunities to explore their attitudes, and to build inter-personal skills and self-esteem.

Sex education should always be sensitive to the developmental stage of the individual, and to her personal sexual history. There are several methods of teaching sex education; the most effective tend to be the participatory models. Sex education needs to be backed up by a whole-school environment in which the values and approaches it teaches are reinforced, and pupils are provided with other opportunities to gain information and advice.

The school nurse may have an important role in assisting teaching staff in devising and carrying out the sex education programme. It is important that the school nurse is adequately trained before embarking on this work.

School nurses will be guided by their professional judgement and experience when making decisions about what is appropriate information for the age and maturity of the pupils they are teaching. Children's questions about sex should, in principle, be answered. To refuse to answer will only exacerbate the situation of misinformation, ignorance, or fear which led to the question being raised in the first place. Children are also likely to be less inhibited than adults, and more explicit in their questions. They are naturally curious about sex. If a school nurse judges that the reply to one child's question would not be appropriate for the whole class, one possible strategy is for her to talk with the child separately after the class. It can be more damaging to children if issues are avoided and adults refuse to answer their questions instead of giving them a straightforward, simple reply.

Children's questions about sex should, in principle, be answered. It can be more damaging to children if issues are avoided and adults refuse to answer questions.

In addition, since the school nurse does not have an academic role, she may be a trusted adult in whom pupils can confide and ask further questions. Many school nurses are also involved outside the school in projects such as safer sex education initiatives in youth clubs and other such out-of-school youth projects.

Government guidance stresses that teachers should tell the parents if a child under 16 comes to them for advice about contraception.[1] Health and medical professionals, including school nurses, are not bound by this ruling, however. The school nurse must decide on the basis of her professional judgement and the child's best interests whether to inform the child's parents. If she deems the young person able fully to understand the implications of the situation, and to be in no danger, and the child is adamant that her parents should not know, then the school nurse may (and should) respect the child's confidence.[4]

In some areas health authorities, trusts, and voluntary organisations run special family planning and sexual health services targeted at young people. School nurses should make sure they are up-to-date with the local provisions, so they can refer children and young people to these services for further help and advice. Often school nurses who also have a qualification in family planning do sessional work in these services, such as special family planning clinics.

14.3 **Support**

Sex education in schools can be a difficult area of work, as it touches on so many personal, and sometimes painful, areas of individuals' lives. In addition, the frequent misunderstandings and media misrepresentations about this work intensify its inherent difficulties. Schools must inform parents of the policy on sex education, but many school nurses and teachers have found it helpful to discuss the content of the sex education programme in more detail with parents. Parents' evenings provide a good opportunity to explain the programme and reassure parents about the framework within which children are learning about sex. Not infrequently parents themselves welcome advice and information on sex and sexual health.

School governors tend to be busy people, and now have a very high level of financial and legal responsibility for the running of the school. So, while they are responsible for drawing up the school's sex education policy, they may not prioritise the issue unless there is a problem. School nurses can be a very valuable resource to governors by contributing to the formation of the policy. Gaining the school governors' and parents' full support for the school's sex education programmes is extremely important, and will help avoid problems arising.

Similarly, a joint approach involving school nurses and teachers means schools can be more flexible in their sex education programmes, and pupils will have access to a number of different staff with a range of roles and expertise for support and advice on sexual matters.

1   Department for Education. Education Act 1993: sex education in schools. Circular no 5/94. May 1994.

2   For a comprehensive review of research studies see: Aggleton P, Baldo M, Slutkin G. Does sex education lead to earlier or increased sexual activity in youth? Geneva: WHO Global Programme on AIDS, 1993.

3   Hutton C. A major impact on how young people learn about sex. AIDS Matters. Issue 13; August, 1993.

4   BMA et al. Confidentiality and people under 16: guidance issued jointly by the BMA, GMSC, HEA, Brook Advisory Centres, FPA and RCGP. January 1994.

SECTION 4

Professional issues

Working with people with HIV and AIDS requires the same high standards of professional practice as any other activity undertaken by health visitors, school nurses and practice nurses. All registered health visitors and nurses owe the same duty of care to clients with HIV/AIDS as to any other. There is absolutely no justification for a nurse or health visitor to refuse to provide care for someone with HIV infection or AIDS, on any grounds.

Confidentiality is of paramount importance to clients affected by HIV/AIDS, and is clearly an issue when the health visitor or nurse is recording information about a client's condition. Health visitors and school nurses who are, or suspect they may be, HIV-infected will have additional concerns, both personal and professional. This section looks in detail at the duty of care owing to clients with HIV/AIDS, the issues of confidentiality and record-keeping, and the requirements on health professionals with HIV infection, and on their colleagues, managers and employers.

15   Confidentiality

CONFIDENTIALITY IS A DUTY owed by all registered nursing professionals to all clients and patients, in all situations. Clause ten of the UKCC code of professional conduct stipulates that it is the individual responsibility of every registered nurse, midwife and health visitor to: 'protect all confidential information concerning patients and clients obtained in the course of professional practice, and make disclosures only with consent, where required by the order of a court, or where you can justify disclosure in the wider public interest'.[1]

With respect to HIV and AIDS, the need for confidentiality is particularly critical. Current routine procedures for completion and storage of health records may need to be reviewed.

Client confidentiality covers not only the HIV status of an individual (or family), but also whether they have been tested, if loved ones are affected by HIV, details about their personal lifestyle, medical condition, sexual and drug using behaviours, and any other information obtained in the course of the health professional's involvement and duties.

HIV/AIDS is still a highly stigmatised condition, and is widely regarded with fear and panic. People who are known to be HIV-positive have experienced extreme forms of discrimination. Individuals closely involved with people with HIV/AIDS, or who are perceived as being at high risk of having HIV infection, have also encountered discrimination.

An HIV/AIDS diagnosis is a serious event in a person's life; most people will need privacy and the opportunity to adapt to the situation. Again, this reinforces the need for absolute confidentiality to be maintained.

It is the individual's right to decide who has access to personal information held about them on their health record, including their HIV status. Breaking confidentiality may not only cause distress to the individual; in the case of HIV/AIDS it can cost a person their job, home and safety. People with HIV have good reason to be concerned about breaches of confidentiality, and this concern may mean clients do not inform a health professional that they are HIV-infected.

The basic principle of confidentiality is that information about clients should only be shared with other health professionals on a 'need to know' basis. Very few health professionals will need to know a client's HIV status in order to provide safe and appropriate care. Universal infection control precautions should be routine, and are more than adequate to prevent risk of transmission to either the health professional or the client.

Health visitors and school nurses may be able to offer important support if they are aware of a client's HIV status, but there is no automatic need to know. It takes time to build a relationship so that the client feels confident to discuss personal issues. Consider how you would feel, and who you would want to know, in a similar situation.

When information about a person's HIV status has been entrusted to a health professional, it should only be shared in the best interests of the individual. Consent to disclosure should always, where at all possible, be obtained, either from the individual or from their guardian or carer. Children's consent should always be sought where they are deemed able to understand the situation. Ideally consent should be specific to each situation, although it may be more practical or necessary to seek general permission when, for example, there is a need to discuss a client with a number of other health and medical professionals in order to devise an appropriate package of care.

It takes time to build a relationship so that the client feels confident to discuss personal issues. Consider how you would feel, and who you would want to know, in a similar situation.

Before deciding to disclose information about a client's HIV status, the health professional must seek answers to the following considerations:

- if providing the information about HIV status is necessary, or will result in direct benefits for the client
- whether there is another way of gaining the same services without revealing HIV status (for example, housing authorities may accept a doctor's note saying that someone has a life-threatening illness without requiring to know the nature of the illness)
- who will be informed, and whether the information will then be shared by that individual with others
- whether the information will be recorded, and whether others will have access to these records
- whether the client will be able to see these records.

The health visitor or nurse may need to find answers to these questions on behalf of their client, and should be careful to protect the individual's confidentiality when doing so. This may include not revealing that they work with anyone affected by HIV. Most of these facts concern general policies on information requirements and confidentiality, and questions about them need not be specific to HIV and AIDS. If an organisation's confidentiality procedures are inadequate, it may be possible to help develop a better policy, either in general or specific to AIDS.

In child protection situations, it is not appropriate auto-

PROFESSIONAL ISSUES | 91

matically to raise the issue of HIV within a family at a case conference.[2] HIV status should only be disclosed in this situation if it is clearly relevant to the safety and well-being of the child. If there is any doubt in her mind, the health visitor or school nurse should discuss the situation with her designated child protection adviser, who will be able to offer confidential guidance. In this situation, the circumstances can be discussed fully in confidence, as it is clearly in the interests of both child and parents.

Often confidentiality is breached by mistake or inadvertently. This can easily happen where the family concerned lives in a small town or village, or within a tightly-knit community such as an immigrant or religious community or cultural group, where people tend to know each other well. It is therefore generally not advisable to reveal that any of your clients have AIDS or HIV, as others may be in a position to guess their identity. It is also important to be mindful of the access clerical assistants,

It is not acceptable to breach confidentiality by giving information to other health professionals unless it is clearly in the best interests of the client and with their knowledge.

receptionists and ancillary staff may have to a person's records. Often training and advice on HIV/AIDS is focused on professional staff, and it is forgotten that the policies should cover all staff within an organisation.

There is clearly no justification for breaking confidentiality to satisfy other people's curiosity. It is also not acceptable to breach confidentiality by giving information to other health professionals unless it is clearly in the best interests of the client and with their knowledge. Surgeons, dentists, gynaecologists and midwives should not be told about someone's HIV status without the client's consent. It is not the role of the health visitor, school nurse or practice nurse to pass on this information. Nor is there any justification for such disclosure on grounds of needing to protect the health of the medical professional concerned. All health and medical professionals should be following universal infection control procedures in their clinical practice.

The most challenging situation can be when a health professional knows, or suspects, that an HIV-positive client is engaging in unsafe behaviour with someone who is unaware of that person's HIV status. In this situation one approach is to discuss the situation with the individual, ensure that they understand about safer behaviour, and explore with them their reasons for not adopting it. By developing strategies together, you may be able to persuade the individual to change their behaviour, or to tell the other person. If such a situation cannot be resolved, and is a cause of concern, the health visitor or nurse should discuss the matter in confidence with her manager. Confrontation rarely works, and will often drive the individual away from contact with the health services.

It can be very hard to keep confidentiality, especially if the situation is professionally or personally stressful. You may feel you need support and want to discuss your concerns with colleagues, or with your partner or close friends. But it is surprisingly easy to identify an individual by the characteristics of their situation. If you need support (and most people do), then speak with your client about the problem. They may be happy to agree on, say, one person with whom you can discuss the case (for example, your manager or clinical supervisor), or you may be able to identify someone completely outside the situation who is unlikely to know the individual(s) concerned, or who can support you without needing to know the details of the situation. Discussing this with the client enables her to keep control over her personal information.

16 Records and record-keeping

HEALTH VISITORS AND school and practice nurses are unlikely to be involved in clinical situations where recording the client's HIV status is critical. The first principle for health visitors, school nurses and practice nurses working with people with HIV/AIDS is that information about an individual's HIV status should not be recorded in child, family or school health records without the client's knowledge and agreement.

Clients must be informed if and how details of their HIV status are to be recorded, and anything recorded should be discussed first and agreed with the client.

Health visitors and school nurses use a variety of health records: the family health record, the school health record and the parent-held child health record, as well as Korner returns. In all situations of record-keeping, the key questions are:

● why does this information need to be recorded?

● who has access to it?

If a client needs specialist care for an HIV or AIDS-related condition, this could be recorded with their permission. But often the nature of the care can be described without using the specific terms 'HIV' or 'AIDS'.

16.1 Family health record

A chronological record of contacts with the family, outlining the care given, should always be kept when there are additional concerns or needs for specialist care. This will ensure continuity of care can be maintained, facilitates the programme of care, and gives the information needed for auditing the caseload. However, as stated above, details of the condition itself need not be specified; simply the care provided. If the family does not wish information about their HIV status to be recorded, reasons for the additional input could be recorded as 'continued care for on-going ill health', or more simply (but less explanatory): 'professional advice and support'.

16.2 Korner statistics

For Korner purposes again there is no need to record the HIV status of a client, but it may be important for the purposes of caseload/workload audit to be able to indicate the additional support a family requires. In many cases codes will only be available to record 'professional advice and support' as above, but if possible health visitors should seek to introduce a code which indicates 'continued care for ongoing ill health'.

16.3 **Child health record**

It is not appropriate to include information about the mother's HIV status on a child's health record. The record relates solely to the child, and information about the parents is only relevant where it impacts directly on the child's physical or mental well-being. Here, as above, it is necessary only to record the factors that are affecting the child's health, the impact on her health and well-being, and the care given; there is no reason to record the parent's HIV status.

Where the child is HIV-positive, again the health visitor should record only the care needs and care given.

If a health visitor is routinely involved with a child whose HIV status is still indeterminate, simply recording the name of the paediatrician who is monitoring the child should be sufficient. The condition for which the child is being monitored should not be recorded (although, if the paediatrician is well known for specialising in AIDS and HIV, this in itself will indicate the child's possible HIV status). It should be born in mind that information which was necessary for the care of a child when an infant may no longer be relevant when the child reaches school age.

16.4 **School health record**

There are often heightened concerns about confidentiality in the school environment. Parents have voiced (unfounded) fears about their child attending a school where other pupils have HIV. The parents or carers of a child with HIV may (with reason) fear their child will be victimised or stigmatised if her HIV status, or that of her parent or parents, is widely known.

As with the child and family health records, there is no clinical necessity to record a child's HIV status in the school health

PROFESSIONAL ISSUES | 95

record, and this information should not be recorded without the consent of the child and parents.

Not all parents will want the school staff (or even the school nurse) to know their child has HIV or AIDS. If a child's HIV status is made known to a school, this information should be treated on a strictly 'need to know' basis, and shared only with the child's, parents' or carers' consent. Not all members of the school staff need to know, and the information will not be relevant to the majority. Those who may need to know, because they are directly involved and because they might usefully provide support to the child, include the school nurse, the head teacher, and the child's tutor or class teacher.

Negative attitudes towards HIV, and discrimination and poor understanding, should be totally unacceptable in any school.

It can be of benefit to the child if these members of the school staff are aware of her HIV status. It will enable staff to offer psycho-social support, if necessary, and staff will understand why a child is frequently absent from school due to illness. It will also enable school staff to protect the child as far as possible from exposure to infections and other illnesses. But all school staff should anyway be practising universal infection control procedures.

Children can be cruel, and staff who know that a child is HIV-positive or affected by AIDS should be alert to general teasing or joking about AIDS among the children, which may be especially hurtful to a child aware of her situation. This kind of behaviour, and games such as 'AIDS tag' should be challenged and discussed with the children. It will be upsetting for the individual child affected by AIDS; but these kinds of negative attitudes towards HIV, and discrimination and poor understanding, should be totally unacceptable in any school.

16.5 **Transfer of records**

When a family moves to a new area, their records pass through many hands and this clearly has implications for maintaining confidentiality. The family may not wish their new health visitor or school nurse to be told of their HIV status.

If a family agrees to this information being disclosed, the health visitor should make direct contact with the new health visitor by telephone, and inform her verbally. Similarly, when a child enters primary school and responsibility passes to the school nurse, information about the child's HIV status should, with the child's and family's consent, be passed on directly and verbally. If it is decided to put the information in writing, the health visitor should always first establish direct contact with the new health visitor or school nurse, and the information should be written on a separate record, and attached to the family or child health record in a separate, sealed envelope.

It may not always be possible to discuss with the client prior to the family's moving whether she wishes the information to be passed on to the new health visitor or school nurse. In such situations the health visitor should ensure that the information about needs (if any) for additional input and support are clearly indicated, but not the reasons for that extra input.

16.6 Practice nurses

Where a patient has been tested for HIV by their GP, the results of the test will, in many cases, be included in the practice notes. Absolute confidentiality and clear guidelines on access to patients' records can be particularly critical in general practice. Practices often serve small, tightly-knit communities, and often employ local people in both clinical and non-clinical areas, who will have access to health records. It is important that the practice has a clear, agreed policy on and procedures for the recording of information about HIV/AIDS, and that all staff working in the practice know and understand the need for confidentiality in such cases.

Patients on the practice list may be required to provide information about their health in general, and about AIDS/HIV in particular, to life insurance and mortgage companies, and sometimes to prospective employers. GPs and practice nurses will often be asked to give this information to the company or organisation concerned. Such information should only be released to the company or organisation on the specific request of the individual concerned, and with their full knowledge and consent.

The patient should know what details have been made available to the company or organisation seeking the information. Information about a patient's HIV status should only be passed on in writing and in confidence; it should never be given verbally, or in response to requests over the telephone; nor should such information be made available in response to requests that do not come via the patient and with her explicit consent.

17 Accountability

THERE HAS BEEN much public anxiety and debate about the dangers to patients from HIV-infected health workers. In fact, throughout the world there has been just one reported – and subsequently disputed – case of an HIV-positive health professional infecting a client in the course of their clinical treatment.[3,4]

There have been several surveys of occupational risks and HIV-infected health workers, and no other cases of transmission from health professional to client have been found. Health workers are, in fact, more likely to acquire infections from a patient than vice versa, as can be seen from the incidence of hepatitis B transmission. The occupational risk of exposure to HIV infection for health workers from clients or patients is also extremely low, and should be absolutely minimal if universal infection control procedures are followed.

The occupational risk of exposure to HIV infection for health workers should be minimal if universal infection control procedures are followed.

Detailed information and guidance about the professional obligations of HIV-positive health workers has been issued by the Department of Health,[5] and, for registered nurses, midwives and health visitors, by the UKCC.[6]

To summarise:

● all health professionals have a professional and legal duty to act in the interests of the client, and to 'do no harm' to the patient/client. This includes taking steps to ensure they do not knowingly expose patients and clients to any infection, including HIV. Infection control procedures which exist to protect health workers from HIV are more than adequate also to protect patients, and should be practised by all health workers, whether they know they are HIV-positive or not

● health professionals who believe they may have been exposed to HIV, in whatever circumstances, must seek medical advice and, if appropriate, antibody testing. Health workers who know they are HIV-positive are required to seek expert medical and occupational health advice and ongoing monitoring. This may result in their transfer to an area of work which does not involve exposure-prone procedures. Those directly involved in exposure-prone procedures (for example, surgery) must seek expert advice, and must not continue to perform such procedures.

Health professionals are not obliged to inform their manager if they are HIV-positive. Some may want their manager to be aware of their situation, and may welcome their support in continuing with their work. HIV-positive health workers may need to take special precautions to avoid other infections. They should not be required to carry out procedures which place them at occupational risk. For example, a health visitor or school nurse who is HIV-positive would be advised not to work with a family where there is active TB. HIV-positive health workers should discuss these risks with their doctor or specialist, who will be able to give detailed advice.

Knowledge of a colleague's HIV status should be treated with the same duty of confidentiality as information about clients. This confidentiality should be respected to the same degree if an HIV-positive colleague has died.

Health professionals are not automatically required to inform managers if they are aware of a colleague's HIV-positive status and the colleague has not disclosed this information to the appropriate authority. As in all such situations, this should only be necessary where the individual's state of health or standards of practice pose a threat to the well-being of patients and clients. The UKCC code of professional conduct makes clear the individual nurse's responsibilities in such situations.

1   UKCC. Code of professional conduct. Third edition. London: UKCC, 1992.

2   HVA. Protecting the child: an HVA guide. London: HVA, 1994.

3   Arnold C et al. The case of the Florida dentist: an unusual mode of HIV transmission. Public Health Laboratory Service. Microbiology Digest 1993; 10, 1. See also NAM for further information.

4   *Sunday Times*. News report. 10 July, 1994.

5   Department of Health. AIDS/HIV-infected health care workers: guidance on the management of infected health care workers. Recommendations of the Expert Advisory Group on AIDS. UK Health Departments; March, 1994.

6   UKCC. Acquired immune deficiency syndrome and human immuno-deficiency virus infection: the council's position statement. Registrar's letter 4/1994.

SECTION

5

Resources

1 Books and manuals

2 Training

3 Health education

4 Sex education

5 General support and resources

Knowledge about HIV and AIDS is constantly developing, and the quantity of available, research-based information is growing rapidly. HIV/AIDS is a relatively recent condition, and the impact on families in the UK is, similarly, a new phenomenon and comparatively rare. Few health visitors and school nurses will therefore have had direct, personal experience of working with clients affected by the disease. Preparation for practice equips the nurse or health visitor with the basic professional skills needed for responding to the care needs of clients with HIV or AIDS. However, practitioners may wish to supplement and extend their basic skills by seeking further information and training in specific skills. This section offers guidance on resources available, and where to find them.

1 Books and manuals

IT WOULD BE IMPOSSIBLE to recommend particular books on HIV and AIDS as there are already so many on the market, and new books are constantly being published.

A good starting point for anyone seeking further information about HIV/AIDS is the *National AIDS Manual (NAM)*. This is the standard reference on HIV and AIDS in the UK. The manual comprises three volumes, regularly up-dated, which provide comprehensive information on the facts about AIDS and HIV, a directory of AIDS-related services and training courses in the UK, and the latest information on the treatment of HIV, trials or new treatments and results of research studies. *NAM* also publishes a monthly newsletter, *AIDS Treatment Update*. These resources are available from *NAM,* Unit 52, Eurolink Centre, 49 Effra Road, London SW2 1BZ.

Information and advice about further reading is also available from the **Terrence Higgins Trust** library, in London (see *General support* below).

A comprehensive resource for clinical information about children and HIV/AIDS is *Guidelines for management of children with HIV infection*, by D.Gibb and S.Walters, published by AVERT, 1993.

2 Training

MANY WORKERS FIND IT helpful to have training in HIV/AIDS issues, to clarify information, provide an opportunity to explore attitudes and feelings about working with people with HIV/AIDS, and develop skills in discussing AIDS-related issues with clients. The **English National Board** (ENB) runs a specific course on 'Care and management of persons with AIDS and HIV-related conditions' (ENB 934). This course is run at over 25 colleges in various parts of the UK. *NAM* includes information about course venues.

There are numerous training packs and resource materials addressing the issue of HIV/AIDS. It is for the individual to decide which best meets her professional needs. One very useful review of teaching/training materials, which provides a good starting point is: *Training AIDS handbook: how to choose, use and develop HIV training resources*, published by the **Health Education Authority**.

3 Health education

THE **HEALTH EDUCATION AUTHORITY** (HEA) provides information to supplement local provision of health promotion and health education materials available from district health promotion units. The main HEA library in London contains a wide range of materials and training packs, and most health promotion units will loan out training packs and videos. The **Terrence Higgins Trust** also produces health education materials, and can sometimes supply or recommend speakers for teaching events. However for those based outside London, it will usually be best to contact the district health promotion unit.

The **Health Education Authority** is based at Hamilton House, Mabledon Place, London WC1H 9TX ☎ 071 278 9528.

4 Sex education

FOR ADVICE AND UP-TO-DATE information and training on sex education and family planning/contraception issues, contact the **Family Planning Association** at 27-35 Mortimer Street, London W1N 7RJ ☎ 071 636 7866.

For information on sex education in schools, national policy and campaigns, and resources and training, contact the **Sex Education Forum**, National Children's Bureau, 8 Wakley Street, London EC1V 7QE ☎ 071 278 9441.

5 General support and resources

ALL HEALTH DISTRICTS WILL have specialist HIV workers, and most will have a district HIV prevention co-ordinator (DHPC). This worker is responsible for co-ordinating HIV prevention work across the district, and will know about other workers and services specialising in HIV/AIDS care and prevention and policies. The DHPC will be a useful local resource for workers seeking training, information and resources. Usually these workers are based in the DHA department of public health medicine or health promotion unit. Health advisers in the local GUM clinic will also be able to put you in touch with people working locally on AIDS/HIV projects.

There may be local voluntary groups working on AIDS/HIV issues, and it can be useful to contact them. They are likely to welcome the professional expertise offered by health visitors and school nurses. Such groups may offer health professionals the opportunity for a greater involvement in local activities, as well as providing individual practitioners with support and encouragement in developing this aspect of their role.

Health visitors and school nurses may want to set up local support groups for community nurses wishing to develop their professional knowledge and expertise in working with HIV/AIDS, or to provide mutual support and informal supervision.

Clients may need advice about contacting local support, information and health care services. The DHPC should be able to provide information on what is available for HIV-positive clients, and those concerned about HIV. National organisations offering help and advice include the **Terrence Higgins Trust** and the **National AIDS Helpline**, who can also refer you on to groups for people with special needs, such as **Positively Women** (for women affected by AIDS/HIV); **Mainliners** (an organisation for people affected by HIV/AIDS), and the **Haemophilia Society**.

The Barnardo's **Positive Options** scheme for children of parents with HIV/AIDS who may need fostering or adoption can be contacted at **Positive Options**, 354 Goswell Road, London EC1V 7LQ ☎ 071 278 5039. Workers from **Positive Options** are also based in other organisations such as **Positively Women** and the **Haemophilia Society**.

The **Terrence Higgins Trust** provides direct support services for people in London with HIV/AIDS, and also offers expert welfare and legal advice. The trust is also a useful resource for health promotion materials. Its library is the largest general AIDS library in Europe, and is open daily Monday to Friday, by appointment with the librarian. Information workers also respond to written enquiries. The **Terrence Higgins Trust** is based at 52-54 Grays Inn Road, London WC1X 8JU ☎ administration 071 831 0330; ☎ helpline (12.00 pm-10.00 pm daily) 071 242 0101.

The **National AIDS Helpline** is a 24-hour, free and confidential telephone helpline, staffed by trained workers. There are also regular helpline sessions in Asian languages, and by Minitel. The helpline provides factual information as well as counselling and support. **National Aids Helpline** ☎ 0800 567 123.

APPENDIX 1

Abbreviations:

AIDS   Acquired immune deficiency syndrome
CDSC Centre for Disease Surveillance and Control
CMV   Cytomegalovirus
CNS   Central nervous system
DHPC District HIV prevention co-ordinator
GI   Gastro-intestinal
GUM   Genito-urinary medicine
HIV   Human immunodeficiency virus
KS   Kaposi's Sarcoma
PCP   Pneumocystis Carinii Pneumonia
PCR   Polymerase chain reaction
PID   Pelvic inflammatory disease
STD   Sexually transmitted disease
WHO   World Health Organisation

APPENDIX 2

Glossary

Antibody positive

This is sometimes used to describe a person who has received a positive result to the HIV antibody test, indicating that she or he has been exposed to the virus and is infected with HIV. People are also referred to as 'body positive' and 'HIV-positive'.

AZT

This is the first anti-retroviral therapy licensed in the UK. This type of drug aims to stop HIV from replicating by blocking the mechanism which transcribes RNA to DNA in the infected cell. AZT has been proven to have some effect in people with AIDS. However the Concorde trial in asymptomatic HIV–positive people suggests that there is no long–term added benefit in beginning treatment before a person has developed symptoms.

CD4 cells

These are also known as 'T-helper cells'. T cells are essential to the proper functioning of the immune system. The CD4 type of T cell is particularly affected by HIV, which inhabits its nucleus and destroys it. Monitoring trends in the numbers, percentage, ratio and/or function of CD4 cells is an essential component of clinical care for people with HIV.

CD8 cells

These are also known as 'T-suppressor cells'. Since HIV reduces the number of CD4 cells, the ratio of suppressor to helper T cells can become reversed. When this happens there are more cells suppressing the activity of the immune system than helping it.

Cunnilingus

Oral sex performed on a woman; licking the clitoris, vulva and vagina.

Factor VIII

A product which facilitates blood clotting. Most Factor VIII is produced from plasma acquired from hundreds of donors. As this is a product, not whole blood, it can be heat-treated to de-activate pathogens, including HIV. Many people with haemophilia became infected with HIV before heat treatment was introduced. Synthetic Factor VIII is in development.

Fellatio

Oral sex performed on a man; sucking and licking a penis.

Femidom

The UK brand name for a contraceptive barrier method and STD prophylaxis for women, also known as a vaginal pouch or 'female condom'.

Haemophilia

A blood clotting disorder. There are different types, of which Type A is the most severe. Without treatment people with haemophilia have a shortened life expectancy as simple bruising can lead to haemorrhage. Haemophilia is genetically acquired from the mother and overwhelmingly affects males.

HIV-positive

A positive result to the HIV antibody test, indicating that a person has been exposed to the virus and is infected with HIV. People are also referred to as 'antibody positive' and 'body positive'.

Inter-partum

During pregnancy. In terms of HIV this describes infection of the fetus from the mother via the placenta.

Intra-partum

During delivery. In terms of HIV this describes infection of the infant from the mother via cervical secretions or blood at the time of childbirth.

Non-oxynol 9

A chemical contained in some spermicidal lubricants. This chemical de-activates HIV in test tubes, and may have some effect against HIV in humans. However it can cause sensitivity, which increases vulnerability to infection.

Opportunistic infection

An infection which has the opportunity to cause damage or disease because the immune system is compromised and consequently the body cannot respond efficiently. When an individual with HIV develops an opportunistic infection, they are diagnosed with AIDS.

p24 antigen

This protein of HIV can be measured, although the test is expensive and not extremely sensitive. Positive detection of antigen (antigenaemia) indicates that the virus is replicating and suggests that the HIV-positive person may be particularly infectious.

Polymerase chain reaction

This is a test which amplifies the DNA in a virus. With HIV this can be an accurate test for the virus before antibodies are detectable. However it is expensive and not very sensitive.

Retrovirus

A virus which stores its genetic message in the RNA. This has to be transcribed to DNA, using the enzyme reverse transcriptase, before becoming established within the DNA of a host cell.

Risk assessment

The process of analysing the level of risk involved in past, current or future behaviour, leading to decisions about how and whether to reduce these risks. In the context of HIV this can include assessing the likelihood that sexual partners have contracted HIV.

Sero-conversion

The period of time during which antibodies (to HIV) are developing. During this time the serum 'converts' from giving a negative result to an HIV antibody test to giving a positive result.

Window period

This describes the period of time after HIV infection has occurred, when sero-conversion is occurring and HIV antibodies cannot yet be detected in the blood. This period is generally taken to be no more than three months, although where exposure is highly probable HIV antibody tests should be repeated six months after the event to confirm a negative result.

Works

The syringe, needle and other paraphernalia used to inject drugs.